D1333410

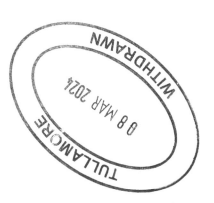

Contents

Though butter's elusive: Oh! Where does it go!
        And bacon a meagre selection:
Though sugar may vanish ere ever we know –
        We've stores of affection.
Whatever it is make this old world go round.
        Whatever may cause indigestion!
Of one thing there will never a surfeit be found,
        Nor excess—of affection.
So in spite of the threatened ration of food.
        We can surely resist sad dejection.
So long as we wisely absorb all the good
        To be had –from affection.

R.H.W.

Edinburgh, 18th November, 1939

Introduction

ESTHER RANTZEN

The past is a foreign country, said LP Hartley, they do things differently there. Even when you have lived through it, it's hard to recapture the real flavour. The second world war years have become a treasure trove regularly plundered by documentary film-makers, and the background for classic films. They created a monochrome image of that time, drained of colour. Sometimes this black and white stereotype makes it difficult to remember that the bomb sites, the Spartan way of life actually happened here, in living memory, in a Britain which has changed radically in the last seven decades. But the letters to newspapers, lovingly collected and arranged in this fascinating book, add the colour and reality, and give us a vivid glimpse of everyday life during those hard years during and soon after the war.

I was born in 1940, so I can just remember the blackout and the gas-masks, the sound of air-raid sirens, and the taste of rose-hip syrup and the thick, heavy malt mixture which was fed to me on an enormous spoon. Some doctors tell us now that the war-time diet was better for us because we had more fish than meat, and very little butter, few eggs. I can still remember the disgusting taste of powdered egg. And I would find it very hard now to give up the fresh fruit and vegetables I've become used to.

My family had moved out of London which they realized would be a constant target for German bombs to a little country town, Berkhamsted in Hertfordshire. There was a pony in the paddock, and a wide lawn sprinkled with daisies. But my father had constantly to travel back to London spending the weekdays there. He was in a 'reserved occupation' working for the BBC which of course was vital during the war, he told me many years later that he was one of the few BBC executives who knew which pieces of music beamed out to Nazi-occupied Europe had particular messages for the extraordinarily courageous members of the Resistance there. And he was almost caught in two bombs in London, one which hit the BBC's Broadcasting House. He described how it brought down the ceiling, but the staff were safe, sheltering under a heavy metal table. That must be why my family in Berkhamsted organised regular drills hiding under the dining-room table, and putting on the hot, uncomfortable rubber gas masks which looked oddly like elephant faces. I hated the gas masks, but I can't remember ever being frightened in spite of the danger my parents must have been aware of, and there is no fear reflected in the letters to the newspapers reprinted in this book. The British had too much pride. They would complain about the food, and the queueing, but never about shouldering the responsibility of defending the world against Hitler and his hideous regime, and the lives that were sacrificed to save families like mine.

There is a great deal of detail about food rationing in these pages which resonates with my own memories of those tough times. I feel no nostalgia for spam, the slices of meat that looked like bright pink plastic, or the equally strange fish called 'snook'. I can still see the piles of soft, wrinkled apples we wrapped in newspaper when I was a toddler in the hope they would last all winter. They didn't. And unlike toddlers today we had no oranges at all, and of course no bananas. In fact, I can recall the first time I tried to peel a banana after the war in 1946, and felt so crushed when it was pointed out to me that you can pull down the yellow rubbery skin in strips, instead of opening it up like a parcel, as I had.

But as a child I had no idea what it was like to make do and mend, and try to feed a family on the sparse rations we were allowed. I do remember my parents talking nostalgically about the cream and meringues they had enjoyed in the enchanted land they lived in 'before the war'. Such luxuries seemed so far away, my party food made by my mother consisted of the 'junket', thin, pale, slightly bitter, with a light dusting of nutmeg. How fascinating to learn that during the war Dr Edith Summerskill, the Minister in charge of Food, had decided that the only delicacy to be allowed to remain unrationed would be haggis, not, it seems because otherwise the Scots would revolt, but due to its ingredients, which are best not dwelt upon.

I dimly realized when I was little that there was something wicked called the 'black market' because I remember my mother complaining about it, but until I read the letters in this wonderful collection, I didn't know how pernicious it was. It seems that the black market even tainted the tinned meat so that some of it was really unlabelled horseflesh, an early echo of the recent scandal of horse hamburgers . But did the war-time butchers really eke out scarce chickens with starlings? How could they? And the interminable queues that these letter writers describe, having to wait three or four hours for a few scraps of meat, or the one egg per week. I feel ashamed at ever complaining at waiting a moment or two for my turn at the checkout, when our supermarket shelves flaunt the abundance of food from every continent, in season and out.

As you read this kaleidoscope of images from the forties and fifties, you will find certain ones stay in your memory. For me, it is the revelation that strong underpinnings were even more important to the morale of Britain's women than good food. As a lady who describes herself as 'an ordinary housewife and mother' writes, it would do wonders for her vigour and confidence if she could have 'a good corset', 'decent elastic' for her underwear and 'four really strong elastic suspenders.' I wonder how she would feel about tights and lycra? I remember watching my own grandmother forcing her cuddly body into a 'good corset' with its ferocious bones and lacing that turned her into a pillar of respectability. The 'elastic suspenders' were attached to this formidable garment, and over them went satin bloomers down to her knees, into which she tucked her hankies. A sternly sturdy race, the British women of the 40's and 50s.

But it's not all about fortitude. There is compassion also in these letters. One of the most striking is a letter from Lester Smith from Hastings and St Leonards, writing in 1946, fresh from a war which had put the whole world in danger, when war crimes were committed on an industrial scale. With these memories vivid in his mind, Mr Smith still recommends that we should give up our meagre sweets ration 'as a Christmas present to the German children who are living in such misery in the British zone. We cannot saddle these little ones with the responsibility for the Nazi regime. Cannot we help in this way to brighten their Christmas?' Reading the humanity in Mr Smith's letter, and the courage and stoicism reflected in so many of the others, they brighten and illuminate this recent chapter in our national past. It may be a foreign country, but it's one we can be amused by, startled by, but above all, we have to admire.

Ten little busy buddies standin' in a line,
Yin got her cookin' fat—an' then there was nine.

Nine little busy buddies—what a weary wait!
Yin got a pund o' saut—an' then there was eight.

Eight little busy buddies—yin o' them was leavin',
Laden up wi' this and that—then there was seeven (sic).

Seeven (sic) little busy buddies—up tae a' the tricks,
'A box o' matches, if you please'—an' then there was six.

Six little busy buddies very much alive,
Yin went aff wi' cookin' aipples—then there was five.

Five little busy buddies cursin' at the war,
Yin was wantin' mealie puddin's—then there was four.

Four little busy buddies weary as could be,
Yin got something in a bottle—then there was three.

Three little busy buddies—'Now, mum, what for you?'
'Half a pund o' potted heid'—then there was two.

Two little busy buddies—now we'll soon be done,
Yin forgot her ration book—then there was one.

One little busy buddies—wasn't it a sin?
Waitin' for her treacle—an' the treacle a' din.

W. R.

Dundee, 9th October, 1944

1

Ration Fashion

Over a quarter of Britons were required to wear a uniform during wartime which put a colossal strain on the textile industry. Civilian clothes had to be sacrificed. Each clothing item was allocated a 'point' value based on how much labour and material went into the item's manufacture. Women's shoes cost five points, whereas men's shoes cost seven points.

Every adult was initially allocated 66 points a year, but this allocation dwindled as the war progressed. In late 1945 only 24 points were issued. Black-out material and parachute silk subsequently found their way into dresses.

The government-sponsored Utility clothing range introduced durable subsidised clothes to the public while the rich could afford to buy more stylish, and longer lasting, bespoke outfits. There was considerable frustration with getting adequate clothing for children and many housewives faced ruinous school uniform expenses.

Making the Best Use of Wool

SIR – My son, who is in the R.A.F., has just been on leave and brought with him his woollies to be washed. Most of them were familiar, having been knit by myself, but one strange article I was told was supposed to be a helmet. It looked like a cross between a sweater for Teddy Brown and a foot-muff. I asked if he used it, and he said, 'Yes, we put it on the barrage balloons on cold nights.' There must be hundreds being sent out like this one, absolutely no use to the lads who receive them, except as a joke. I have pulled the thing out and am knitting a pair of socks with the wool, so this one won't be wasted.

[A feature of the knitting done for the Forces has been its high quality. There are bound to be some 'throw outs' among the comforts sent in to the various knitting circles. This is the first instance of this kind, however, that has been brought to the notice of the *Evening Post*.—Ed.]

GRATEFUL MOTHER

Leeds, 27th July, 1940

Uniformly Disgusted

SIR – With reference to the subject of school uniforms I have been rather disgusted at the long list of clothes required by the children attending the Nottingham secondary schools. When parents have to find between £5 and £10, for uniform alone, it is no wonder that clever children are often barred by financial reasons, from continuing their education.

Surely the uniform could be cut down to more reasonable proportions. All that was necessary for the girls' department of the old High Pavement School was a gym frock, white blouse, gym shoes, and a hat with school badge. One wonders if those responsible are thinking more of the uniform than the reason why secondary schools were first started. That was to give children of working people a better chance in life.

PRACTICAL

Nottingham, 6th November, 1940

Darn Girls

SIR – The rationing of clothes is bound to have at least two good effects. First, it will give to all, both poor and rich, an equable position as regards the purchase of clothes, though not as to the price paid. Secondly, it will force the younger generation of the female sex to practise the almost lost art of needlework, especially that part of it which is included in the comprehensive term of 'mending.'

No more will the would-be fashionable young woman be able to purchase stockings galore, casting away those that require darning into the ragbag. I know of many modern misses who openly boast that they purchase a pair of stockings every week because it is too much trouble to darn the holes.

T. G. PHILLIPS

Cheltenham, 4th June, 1941

Expectant Clothes

SIR – How is the expectant mother going to manage now clothes rationing is in force? I know that baby clothes are not included in the rationing scheme, but the majority of mothers prefer to make their own garments. I have made a rough estimate and to provide just the necessary garments, nothing to spare, I find it will take up 35 coupons. If I have to take these from my own 66 coupons I shall only have the balance of 31 for my own wardrobe for a year.

[This point is already under official consideration, with others. The baby gets a Clothes Coupon Card as soon as he is born, and it is suggested that a mother can repay herself out of these coupons.—Ed.]

M.P.

Portsmouth, 4th June, 1941

Flying Colours

SIR – The female sex will feel the pinch of the clothes rationing more so than the men, because as every woman knows, they like to appear smartly dressed and rightly so, but the problem of dress is their affair, and I am certain they will overcome this difficulty with flying colours.

SEA SAW

Selkirk, 17th July, 1941

Maid Up

We hear a great deal about the rationing of clothes, but has sufficient thought been given what it means to maids, who have to buy two sets of uniforms? Employers should be willing to let the girls wear what they like, and dispense with the wearing of uniforms until at least after the war.

MAID'S POINT OF VIEW

Nottingham, 30th August, 1941

Classist Clothes

SIR – The more one analyses the various coupon and rationing schemes, the more it becomes clear that there is lack of equality about them. They give an unfair advantage to those with means. They can purchase any article of wearing apparel of the very best quality which will outlive three or four times anything that is bought by the ordinary man with limited means. The food rationing appears a glaring example of how not to ration food. A small section of the community can spend three to five shillings or more two or three times a day on a lunch, dinner of supper at an hotel. Consequently, their families have extra rations. How many men or women employed in industry can afford to do this?

H. E. TURNER

Nottingham, 17th February, 1942

Girls of the W.A.A.F.

SIR – Last week I visited my young daughter—a recruit in the W.A.A.F. At this station, somewhere in England, thousands of girls learn drill and deportment and good comradeship. One wakes in the morning to the sound of marching feet, to commands given in girls' voices, clear and crisp.

I talked with many other companions, and noted the same spirit of cheerful determination.

Among the girls who had been in the Service for some time and are engaged in training the 'rookies' was a wistful longing for just a few coupons for civilian clothes to add to the enjoyment of leave. 'I have been in nearly two years,' a young woman in 'Admin' said to me, 'and our civvies do want cheering up a little. If we could have just a few, a new frock, stockings, and a lighter pair of shoes, it would be grand.'

Others were hoping that when posted they would be put as near home as possible, with a little complaint that a Scottish girl had been sent to Cornwall while a Cornish girl doing the same work was sent to Scotland.

Some had a sigh over the rather heavy meals, and the hope that as salads got cheaper they would be given more. All very simple requests, and I feel sure that all will be done that is possible to fulfil them.

A MOTHER

Leeds, 25th April, 1942

Feeling the Pinch

SIR – We are a family of six, three are children under thirteen, and although I make almost all of our clothing, coats, trousers, etc., I find it a very hard struggle to manage on the coupons. Neither my husband or myself have had much in the way of new clothing since rationing began, as our coupons go mostly on the children, the eldest boy especially. During the last three month I have bought him two pairs of shoes (14 coupons), two shirts (10 coupons) and material for two pairs of trousers (12 coupons), three pairs of socks (nine coupons) making a total of 45 coupons. When the new period begins I have to buy him an overcoat or material for the same. As he is man's size, 5ft. 6in. tall, I suppose that will run into about 16 coupons, leaving few for any other necessities which always needs renewing. I need new towels, etc., this period, so I will have to go easy on the other coupons to buy these. If we only had a few more coupons for household use it would be a great help. I have tried advertising for necessities, but have been unlucky each time.

M. PALMER

Portsmouth, 28th July, 1943

Home Guard Comforts

SIR – I have noted that the President of the Board of Trade is now proposing to force members of the Home Guard to surrender four clothing coupons in the next issue on the ground that the wearing of the uniform saves wear and tear on civilian clothes.

Bearing in mind that a Home Guard is prohibited from wearing his uniform at any time other than when on parade or on night duty, I fail to comprehend where the saving on civilian clothing comes in. I am aware, however, that the majority of the Home Guard have had to use some of their coupons for the purchase of thick socks for wear with army boots, and that the officers are even worse off, as they have to purchase khaki shirts and ties also.

J. W. C. WHITE

Portsmouth, 4th August, 1943

Nudism

SIR – Rationing does not always work out as equality of sacrifice. So far as perishable goods are concerned the scheme works well enough, but in the matter of clothes it is different.

A slender purse could meet my modest winter requirements—one overcoat, one pair shoes, two pairs socks, and two pairs pyjamas. Total coupon cost—47, 47 from 24 you cannot, as we used to say in the arithmetic class.

Perhaps I am greedy. Perhaps night attire is no longer being worn. In my case it cannot be worn much longer.

DALTON NUDIST.

Dundee, 10th January, 1944

Austerity Suit

SIR – The ban on turn-ups and the restriction on the number of pockets had, the President of the Board of Trade asserted, had a depressing effect. Most men don't mind wearing old clothes. Those who really care about such things have never had to sacrifice turn-ups (is that news to the Minister?) Personally, I don't count it an excessive hardship to be reduced to eight pockets. And even that restriction would worry no one who really wanted more. If there is any depression among males, it surely is caused by the low allotment of coupons.

Tomorrow a man will have 20 to keep him going for the next half-year. For myself, I want a pair of shoes and two pyjama suits are a crying necessity. What do I care if the Minister has legalised turn-ups and no-limit pockets at 26 coupons per suit? How can a man buy a 26-coupon suit with 20 coupons?

GROUSER

Dundee, 31st January, 1944

Children Need More Clothes

SIR – I think it is about time more clothing coupons were issued to children, babies particularly. They receive supplementary coupons, it is true, but these go nowhere. I have found it difficult managing on my own coupons, because my kiddies outgrow their clothing as fast as I buy it. Coupons have to be given for tiny socks, shoes, and so on, which I think is disgraceful.

SOLDIER'S WIFE

Cheltenham, 15th September, 1944

Sock It to Them

SIR – We read of soldiers in Italy fighting in ragged or no socks, and asking for socks and coupons. We have also read of the Government placing orders for demobilisation clothing.

Surely socks, if nothing else, could be sent to our men *now*. It must be cold comfort for those in the mud to know they will have dry socks to come home to, if they are climbing mountains under shell-fire without socks, and with full battle kit strapped about their bodies.

W. R. BIRCHLEY

Cheltenham, 17th October, 1944

Higher Ears

SIR – I have read some letters which have appeared in your paper during the last few days concerning the question of the provision of socks for the soldiers in Italy. I should like to set their minds—and hearts—at rest.

The soldier obtains his marching socks from the unit with which he is serving. His unit obtains these socks 'on indent' from the services which supply a British Army. If things should go wrong—and socks to the infantry are always a serious matter—the officer must see his C.O. and quarter-master about it. Complaints will then be made to superior authority.

Such complaints—especially about a matter like socks—might even get to the ears of the higher commanders of an Army.

OFFICER FROM ITALY

Cheltenham, 20th October, 1944

Back in Black

SIR – We are all rejoicing over the permission of the Home Secretary to remove the black-out.

Much to no doubt will find its way to the salvage dumps; some will be useful to the housewife—one does not contemplate the existence of a housemaid nowadays—and will serve to rub the floors or polish the brass. Some of the lighter brands, sateen or cotton rep, having developed a tendency to tear if it is looked at, can still be used for dust-sheets which need only be flung lightly over the furniture on turning-out days (if such exists in these troubled times).

But in institutions and clubs and shops and offices, there

hang yards and yards of perfectly sound curtains, and one is haunted by the question, 'What will become of all this valuable material?' Through Red Cross appeals are made daily in the papers for the distressed Belgians, or Poles, or Greeks in need of clothes. Each window would provide a complete black dress for a French or Belgian woman—and black is always in favour abroad.

LILIAN M. FAITHFULL

Cheltenham, 13th December, 1944

Larger Ladies

Regarding clothes rationing and inability to obtain ladies' dresses above ordinary W size such as WX and OS, this is a great worry and anxiety to the trade, not only to retailers, but equally so to wholesalers and manufacturers. We have been beaten at being unable to obtain supplies from manufacturers. The chief trouble is the ridiculously small allowance of coupon value. Larger women must be clothed as others. If larger sizes are cut and made there is very soon a great loss of coupons to makers owing to the amount allowed for each piece of material. I took up and explained about the amount of material taken for men's trousers turn-ups, pockets and leg width, and was later gratified by the allowance duly made for same. My attention is now just as keen on behalf of ladies, and I am appointed a delegate to attend the annual conference of National Federation of Credit Traders.

W. M. SHAW, NOTTINGHAM, CREDIT TRADERS' ASS.

Nottingham, 24th May, 1945

Swanky Yankies

SIR – May I, as an Englishman's wife, say I think it very unfair that girls who have married Americans should be given extra coupons to buy more clothes before sailing. Do they need them as much as we women who are not going to America? They will have more chance of getting what they want when they land on the other side. I read an account of one young bride who had 16 towels given her, also sheets and blankets as gifts.

I myself have patched and darned until I shall now have to patch the patches. In fact, it is a nightmare to all of us. If any coupons are to be found, let it be for English women, who have worked very hard to keep the home front going.

PATCHES

Nottingham, 13th October, 1945

Clothing Needs

SIR – I am just an ordinary housewife and mother, and like all the rest of us, I am rather tired of coping with rations and the lack of variety in food. But I really believe I should go to it with renewed vigour and confidence if I could have a good corset, some decent elastic for my underwear, and four really strong elastic suspenders. It would be mental as well as material support.

HOUSEWIFE

Leeds, 30th January, 1946

Troublesome Corsets

SIR – Supply of more and better corsets is pressed for in a petition to Sir Stafford Crips, President of the Board of Trade, which is being prepared by Councillor Mrs R C Maples, of Sheffield.

The Petition states it is simply impossible to wear the present utility corset with any comfort, that for middle-aged women good corsets are absolutely necessary, and that women are suffering in health because they cannot get comfortable corsets.

ANONYMOUS

Dundee, 3rd February, 1946

At Home

SIR – I have a husband, have two children at school, and have given up my coupons time after time so that they could go out respectably dressed. Would it not have been wiser to have given us 26 coupons for the spring, when everyone wants some clothes, and 14 in September? We can always make our old winter coat do another winter. They talk about wanting more children, while mothers give up their food ration to keep the family fit, and now they have to sit in the house for the want of clothes.

AGEING WITH WORRY

Dundee, 23rd February, 1946

Demobbed Farce

SIR – A demobbed serviceman is to get an extra 26 coupons if demobbed after June 13, 1945. Why? A demobbed man gets 50 coupons, plus a number of coupons in a ration book, in addition to one raincoat or overcoat, one lounge suit, one pair shoes, one shirt, two collars, tie, two pairs socks (value 74 coupons). The only thing he doesn't get in demob outfit is underwear, but he can keep his service issue, so he is not quite destitute in this respect. Therefore, 90 demob coupons, plus current issue, will more than double demob outfit, so it seems to me senseless to grant 26 more coupons.

Take the case of a demobbed servicewoman. She gets 90 coupons, plus 35 in lieu of man's demob outfit, and number valid in current ration book. On August 1 a demobbed servicewoman will get 176 coupons. Does she need the extra 26, making 202 coupons altogether?

In view of above facts, I think most civilians will agree the extra 26 to demobbed personnel is a farce, and would have been better distributed amongst civilians, or given to the housewife to replenish her linen cabinet.

SARKLESS

Dundee, 21st June, 1946

Makers of Corsets

SIR – Approximately 6.000.000 yards of government surplus cloths have been diverted to the manufacture of corsets. There is some shortage of skilled labour in the industry, but firms are being encouraged to deconcentrate where the result would be to increase the rate of production.

MR J. W. BELCHER

Leeds, 21st May, 1946

Kidnapped Corsets

SIR – Does the public know that the Board of Trade is prepared to receive applications for licenses from traders who wish to import various goods from any country? Import licenses will be granted for perambulators, wellingtons, corsets and brassieres, vacuum flasks, football cases, enamelled ware, brooms, brushes, elastic scissors, and so on.

All these lines are in great demand by the public and are at the present time being manufactured in this country, but mainly for export only. I am completely at a loss to understand why goods manufactured in Britain are stopped from being sold in Britain, while at the same time licenses are being granted to import the same class of goods from abroad. With import duty and purchase tax, what a square deal for the British public!

C. M. GLANVILLE

Cheltenham, 19th November, 1946

Draper Decisions

SIR – I am a draper and occasionally I get fully-fashioned stockings, usually three pairs. Who should have them? Should I let them go to the first three customers who ask for them; should I let them go to customers who are in and out of my shop practically every day but never buy a pair of stockings, yet think they are entitled to fully-fashioned; or should I let them go to the customers who, although they buy

little else, buy my mock-fashion, which, by the way, I have to
buy, as the only means of ever getting any fully-fashioned?

SMALL DRAPER

Leeds, 25th March, 1947

No Nylons No Work

SIR – The British peoples pride themselves on being 'level
headed'—not given to panic nor easily stampeded. Potato
rationing was scheduled for introduction last year, but owing
to the fuss created by the British Housewives League over
bread rationing it was deemed dangerous to attempt it then.
The best answer was shown recently by 200 factory girls, who
struck or nylons. No nylons, no work. They got their nylons.

W. H. SPOOR

Plymouth, 14th November, 1947

Kid's Size

SIR – I am the mother of three children, and I think the
reason so many children are wearing raincoats in winter is
because they are not given sufficient coupons to purchase an
overcoat as well. I deeply resent the implication that parents
of children who are wearing raincoats in the winter are using
their children's coupons for their own clothing. Personally I
am tired of searching shops at sale-time for coupon
reductions, and weary of trying to keep the whole family
warm and tidy on totally inadequate coupons.

MARGARET FOSTER

Leeds, 31st January, 1948

Shorts in School

SIR – In reference to school uniforms during the war, several
public schools made 'shorts' the official dress for boys up to
16, and in some cases optional after that age. Most of the boys
preferred them to long trousers. This style is more

comfortable, healthier and smarter, besides saving cloth and coupons.

H. DIXON

Leeds, 12th March, 1948

Back to School

SIR – Surely the need for a canteen at Naunton Park is not greater than the need for accommodation. Why build a canteen when children attending Prestbury School are so overcrowded that one class has to take lessons in the Church House, and when that is required for other purposes the children have to go out?

The existing playground is so disgraceful that during the wet weather the younger children slip over in the mud. During the wet spell last year, I had to change all my child's clothes, every day, as they were wet through. Why is this disgusting state of affairs allowed to continue? While on the subject I suggest that a much larger sign indicating 'School' is placed in Bouncers-lane. Most motorists seem to consider this narrow stretch of road as out of the 30-mile limit.

PARENT

Cheltenham, 26th May 1949

Cheltenham Frumps

SIR – If the designer who started the 'New Look' had the misfortune to come to Cheltenham and saw what he had started when he instigated this fashion, he would be horrified, for it is here that one sees the most fantastic styles and weird-looking garments which appear to have been made from discarded Army blankets or disused curtain material.

I think it is due largely to the fact that Gloucestershire people on the whole are slow-witted, non-progressive, and very easily-pleased. Give the one section of Cheltenham a bath chair and a Town Hall concert, and the other a cinema, a glass of beer, and a football pool, and nobody knows or cares whether or not it was Truman who lost the South African election or Smuts who is premiere of Australia. It would certainly do no harm if Cheltenham's frumps really decided to make the most of it.

BOURNEMOUTH BELLE

Cheltenham, 5th June, 1948

2

Pet Peeves

In the summer of 1939 an air-raid precaution pamphlet urged: 'If at all possible, send or take your household animals into the country in advance of an emergency.' It went on to say: 'If you cannot place them in the care of neighbours, it really is kindest to have them destroyed.'

The advice resulted in the death of 750,000 pets within one week of the start of the war, a tragic fact for a nation of animal lovers. If one rejected the recommendation, the next hurdle for pet lovers to cross was feeding pets 'off the ration'. Feeding pets could often prove tricky and attracted the ire of those who viewed pets as a frivolous drain on national resources. The debate between pet puritans, who urged for the destruction of all pets, and dog-lovers, who sang the praises of pets, raged throughout the war.

Dinner for Two

SIR – May I reply to 'Fair Play in War Time' who in answer to 'Old Timer' states that 'the food that is wasted on dogs is absolutely wicked'? I wonder why these dog-haters want to live themselves. Why in the name of all that is good can food given to a dumb animal be wasted? There is more food thrown away than that given to our noble friend.

There are many dogs who share their master's meals. I had a cat not long ago and I used to share my meals with it and also take home scraps for it. Where is the waste?'

DOG & CAT LOVER

Cheltenham, 3rd August, 1940

In the Black-Out

SIR – Will you give me space to draw attention to what I consider adds to the difficulty and danger of the black-out? Firstly, people carrying umbrellas are a nuisance. Secondly, people with dogs on a long leash cause considerable trouble. The leash trips others. Better to let the dogs run about. They have sufficient sense to keep clear of pedestrians' feet. Girls who walk along arm-in-arm are a third nuisance. I have met no fewer than four of them walking in this fashion. You dodge one and run into the others! The Golden Rule is especially applicable to the black-out. When people think of others conditions will be improved.

SOUTER

Selkirk, 16th January, 1941

Four Million Unhygienic Saboteurs

SIR – Your gossip-writer tells us of the female saboteur who takes her dog to raid the food bins. This deliberate weakening of the national effort should be made a punishable offence.

In effect, the same sort of thing is going on in something like half the homes of this country. We are urgently asked to save bones, pig food, fuel, and so on, but a large proportion of this is consumed by dogs.

The dog population being, so I read, four millions, it is easy to calculate the vast weekly consumption of bones, human food, pig and poultry food. Also there is the fuel for cooking. This applies in a lesser degree to cats.

The question is, are these conditions to continue? Can the reputed qualities of the dog—'good companions' and so on—which are known only to their respective owners, be weighed against the need for shipping space and the risk to our seamen's lives?

Something drastic should be done to remove this serious obstacle to victory, and at the same time make the streets cleaner and more hygienic.

FOUR MILLION DOGS TO FEED

Cheltenham, 25th August, 1942

Dogs and Cats Help to Win the War

SIR – In reply to 'Four Million Dogs to Feed', his letter is not only unkind, but offensive. The writer states that dogs consume human food. This of course is not correct, how on earth could a dog be kept on this small meat ration, even were we willing to give it to the dog? Dogs are fed on meat which is unfit for human consumption. We buy this meat for our dogs, and there is always plenty available in several of the shops. Our dogs are never allowed bones. If any people cannot afford to buy food for their dog and to feed it properly, it should be taken to the R.S.P.C.A , in Knapp-road, where it could be painlessly destroyed in the lethal chamber.

Let the writer ponder for a moment on the useful work dogs and cars are doing to help us win the war. Taking dogs first: useful guards, leading the blind, invaluable to the shepherd, an absolute necessity in shooting and destruction of vermin. As for the cats, they do a marvellous job of work in destroying rats and mice, both of which are death on our food stuff.

I agree with you correspondent in what he or she says about the pollution of the pavements by dogs. In any case, there is legislation to deal with this.

Col. E. L. DU DOMAINE, R.S.P.C.A CHELTENHAM

Cheltenham, 31st August, 1942

Pests

SIR – The statement that 'dogs are not allowed bones' is just nonsense. Ask any butcher.

We all know of dogs doing something useful. Their numbers are negligible. I am concerned only with the multitude of pets (some may say 'pests'), most of them being allowed to do as they please. But I must not mention the obvious faults of these animals for fear of hurting the tender feelings of their owners.

I would ask Col. Du Domaine to ponder for a moment on the cold fact that war conditions mean the subordination of all private interests. I should not be surprised to hear that 'cats are not allowed milk'. I have noted that the 'marvellous job of work' which these interesting creatures do is to scratch up people's gardens.

FOUR MILLION DOGS TO FEED

Cheltenham, 10th September, 1942

Lassie

SIR – In answer to 'Four Million Dogs to Feed' I feel I, too must take up arms. As the owner of Lassie, the collecting dog of Cheltenham, I should like to point out to the dog-haters of this town that they are very unobservant not to have noted the many useful purposes our dogs serve.

Rats are caught and killed by some very good ratting dogs. To say nothing of the many good dogs who guard lonely women whose husbands are on war-work or active service. There are also the Red Cross dogs, who go out on the battlefield and succour the wounded, where perhaps no human being could move and survive.

Certainly no dog should be fed on food suitable for human consumption. Mine get just scraps, and they look very well on it. Such crimes as raiding the pig-bins should be severely dealt with.

My dog Lassie was my guide dog when I was blind for some months. Also my mother's sight has failed, and she is finding my dogs a great help to her. May our cats and dogs be kept safe from the clutches of people who do not appreciate them.

> OWNER OF 'LASSIE'
>
> Cheltenham, 10th September, 1942

Saboteurs

SIR – Dogs have for some considerable time been a source of nuisance to allotment holders in general. There are far too many owners who just let them out of the house in the morning and hope for the best. Several allotment-holders have complained of the way their seed-beds have been scratched about, and I do think that owners who allow their dogs to roam about are saboteurs of the nation's food efforts. I am not a dog-hater. I have every affection for our dumb friends.

> A. WILLIAMS
>
> Cheltenham, 17th May, 1943

Vermin Destroyer

SIR – Why this controversy over cats and rats? Why do we not give the cat a fair chance to prove herself that she really is the most courageous destroyer of all vermin? Giving her the right to travel, let home be only where she is wanted, cared for, protected, fed and encouraged.

> M. I. COLES
>
> Yeovil, 17th December, 1943

Horses for Fido

SIR – I have no doubt that those of your readers who have domestic pets find considerable difficulty in feeding them. In my view, this is at least partly due to the continued refusal of the Minister of Food to ration horse-flesh, thus bringing about a state of affairs when those who have a taste for it purchase horse flesh in addition to their ordinary meat ration and thus deprive animals of a very necessary food and the only meat they may be given.

E. KEITH ROBINSON, OUR DUMB FRIENDS LEAGUE

Bedford, 18th August, 1944

Taxation on Cats

SIR – With the forthcoming programme of social reform, the cost of which the Chancellor of the Exchequer must have constantly in mind, may I again point out the advantage of a tax on cats? Not only would this raise a very substantial sum, as it is estimated that there are something like 10 million cats in Britain, but it would greatly reduce the number of stray and half-starved cats that can be seen in every town and village in the country. A tax would mean that only those who really want a cat would keep one, and would look after it properly.

E. KEITH ROBINSON

Nottingham, 16th May, 1945

Dogs' Rations

SIR – Owing to the loss of Mr Whatman, the only horse slaughterer in Hastings, dog food has been far more difficult to obtain. No doubt before long supplies will be normal once again. In the meantime there is plenty of dried meat obtainable at pet shops, and this is excellent food for dogs.

S. A. ISLES

Hastings and St Leonards, 5th October, 1946

Dangerous Chokers

SIR – With the reappearance of rubber bands after war-time scarcity, dog owners will be well advised to examine their dogs and cats periodically to ensure that they are not the involuntary wearers of on these dangerous 'chokers'. A rubber band round an animal's throat or tail or leg is quite invisible beneath the coat and will rapidly work its way through the flesh. Canine Defence Clinics have dealt with many cases in which serious wounds have been inflicted in this way. Children are normally the culprits.

R. H. JOHNS, NATIONAL CANINE DEFENCE LEAGUE

Hartlepool, 8th November, 1946

3

Querulous Queues

Integral to the rationing experience was the long, intensely boring queuing experience. Housewives would have to go from shop to shop sometimes waiting hours at a time to get their meagre ration. Children in tow, rain pouring down queuing for rations was the bane of post-war Britain. As one did the rounds visiting the baker, greengrocer, fishmonger, and butcher for unappetising morsels it is easy to see how hatred of rationing set in earliest amongst housewives.

Shop Till You Drop

SIR – I wish to say queues are not the fairest way. We could not get jam, treacle, or any of those things until they were rationed, and now we all have our share regularly.

My husband is a war-worker and served his time in the last war. I have one little boy to go to the shops for me, as I am unfortunate in being an invalid and cannot go myself. Therefore the food I need to help me to get well I cannot get, as the boy is at school all the week, and the shop assistants never seem to have anything for him if he goes after school.

Queues for the 'bus are a different matter. They prevent the old and sick people getting knocked about in the rush and scramble.

If there were equal rations everyone could have a little, and people are not obliged to do their shopping all at the same time. It would also give small traders a chance to keep their business going. Then the old people and invalids would not have to stand in queues until they fainted from exhaustion.

AN INVALID WHO GOES WITHOUT

Cheltenham, 25th July, 1941

Selfish Line Up

SIR – Selfishness is the cause of all this trouble. If all were registered at one shop—grocer, greengrocer and confectioner—shopkeepers would then know what each family got.

We send our orders, which my daughter leaves in the letter-box on her way to war work. We take what is sent. We are being given fair dealing by the shopkeepers. I myself have no time to waste, being left with a middle-class house, with no help, and war work every day from 2 p.m. to 9 p.m., Sundays and weekdays.

L. E. JEFFERSON

Leeds, 5th September, 1941

Old and a Cripple

SIR – Regarding queues, I would like to point out to A Shopper that townspeople as well as colliery people are all out for what they can get and we cannot blame them so long as queues are allowed. My grouse against queues is this; I am old and a cripple and cannot stand in a queue for a little fish or tripe which would be a welcome addition to my ration; and as I have no one to stand for me I must do without for the duration. I dare say there are many more in similar circumstances as myself.

CRIPPLE

Sunderland, 22nd January, 1943

Alphabetical Disorder

SIR – The statement in the *Echo* that 500 Lincoln people

whose names begin with 'A' will have to wait until early next month to collect their ration books seems a little hasty.

If there are persons in the same household whose names begin with different letters of the alphabet, the individual whose initial letter is furthest down in the alphabet should collect all the books when calling for his own, e.g., assuming that Mrs. Brown and Mrs. Smith live together, Mrs. Brown does not queue up with the 'B's but Mrs. Smith queues with the 'S's and collects Mrs. Brown's book at the same time.

C. G. WHITE

Lincoln, 4th June, 1943

Umbrella Death Traps

SIR – A properly-managed town would not allow its High Street to be used as sort of social club by those who hanker after fancy cake etc. Possibly when our Town Council finishes all its internal wars and realizes that there is a world war of more importance it may decide that many local eyesores need attention.

Until then, the innocent passer-by will still be liable to have his or her eye poked out by the queue-held umbrella, which will no doubt educate such a ratepayer to take an even more one-eyed view of candidates when the next election comes along. Close the High Street to all pedestrians and reserve it for queues alone.

ZERO

Bedford, 25th February, 1944

Those Queues

SIR – Why are there more queues in Bedford than many of our big cities? Who is responsible for this and why is it that retailers open their stores only on certain afternoon for the sale of, for instance, tomatoes?

The High Street is a disgrace on Friday afternoons. Women, all of whom are hard worked, have to start queuing about one o'clock, and the shop doors are eventually opened at 2.30 for the sale of fruit which normally could be gathered nearly every day and sold day by day, giving everyone a chance to buy a share. The same applies to cakes. They are all arranged in the windows, but not sold until a big queue has collected.

In cities like Manchester, Warwick and Oxford, one does not see these queues.

A BEDFORD WOMAN

Bedford, 18th August, 1944

Dammed If You Queue Dammed If You Don't

SIR – I cannot understand why some people are complaining of waiting so long for their ration books. In to-night's *Evening News* a Mr. B says he was at the head of the queue and had to wait four hours, and then back in the afternoon for an hour and a half. Can he explain the real reason for so long a wait? I was there Monday at ten minutes to nine, walked in with my books in order, and came out of the gate at 10.15. How is that for quickness? I can only say that if people have to wait so long it is only due to their own neglect in not following instructions.

ANOTHER ONE OF THE Bs

Portsmouth, 21st May, 1943

Endless

SIR – Some days ago it was given out on the wireless that the issue of the new ration books was now practically complete, and that 'only in a few cases' had people had to wait 'more than a few minutes' when calling for their books.

On the appointed day I, in company with a crowd of others, waited at the Town-hall for two hours, 20 minutes. The queue, mostly women—many of them with young children—stretched in what seemed to be a never ending line along the margins of the ballroom, down the stairs, across the landing, up the stairs, across the ballroom floor again, and so to where a team of girls awaited us at the journey's end. This gave one ample time to admire the competence, hard work and patience of the staff; also to wonder, 'Need these things be?'

Even if the war ends next week, there will no doubt be at least one more issue of ration books. May we, therefore, ask the authorities to plan now some better arrangements such as are in operation, evidently, in other towns? Could not voluntary help be called upon, or temporary staff engaged so that the people of Grantham need not again be subjected to such an exhausting and unnecessary ordeal?

H. CHARLESWORTH

Grantham, 30th July, 1943

Complete Prostration

SIR – I congratulate Miss Charlesworth on their letters in protest of the above, and should like to add an account of my experience, which was even more dramatic than theirs!

Like Miss Charlesworth, I queued for considerably more than two hours; but had barely been standing in my place for five minutes, when a young man fell on the floor in a dead faint. Fortunately, he was well away from the stairs, otherwise the consequences might have been serous. He told us later that he had collapsed after waiting for three and a half hours!

I was told later, on good authority, that there were at least 12 such cases of complete prostration. I, too, witnessed many women with young children, and what was even as bad, a considerable number of old age pensioners. The waste of time and the fatigue for all concerned were tremendous.

RUTH QUILTER

Grantham, 6th August, 1943

Thinning Ranks

SIR – I see the Government are to have an inquiry as to why

the population is decreasing. As a mother of three young children my brains are taxed, especially as regards the pudding question—no rice; cornflour, tapioca, custard, very scarce; prunes, figs, apple rings, dried peaches and apricots all non-existent; and no fresh apples. The latest reduction makes it an even harder job. They will maybe get fat on a 'jelly piece' (1 lb. for a whole month), but they will have little reserve for illness.

I have no time to stand in queues—no place for children anyhow—so my menu is further restricted. How an invalid or old body manages I don't know. They have my sympathy.

Instead of sending us American films, it would be more to the point to send the 'G. I. Brides' ships back with tinned fruit or even 'good old spam.'

A DISGRUNTLED HOUSEWIFE

Dundee, 8th February, 1946

Queue Spite

SIR – I wonder if any other of your readers who are, or have been, expectant mothers have been humiliated as I have been when using the 'queue priority' granted to them under rationing conditions. They will risk an upsetting altercation with ignorant women who pass such remarks as 'We didn't get priority,' and 'I don't know how they have the cheek to do it,' etc. It is noticeable that the opposition chiefly comes from women who appear to relish queuing.

HOUSEWIFE

Preston, 28th April, 1947

Call for Ration-book Queue Revolt

SIR – Four years have elapsed since the war ended, but women still have to wait in queues—sometimes for more than two hours—for these pestilential ration books. If we must have ration books, why on earth cannot they be sent through the post in a businesslike way? Why don't the women revolt—

instead of standing there like so many sheep at the bidding of a few swollen-headed bureaucrats? Unnecessary, unwieldy, and stupid.

RICHARD THE FIRST

Cheltenham, 14th April, 1949

Perils of the Queue

SIR – Here are a few examples of the hazards of the course. The housewife whom chance lodges on the square numbered 13 is fortunate. 'Six eggs off the ration. Go on to 29.' Should she be unlucky enough to find herself at number 34 she will be told: 'Points value of sardines increased. Return to 11 at the back of the queue, forfeit three coupons and miss a turn.'

The deadliest hazard of all comes just before the end. Arriving at number 98, with a not greatly depleted ration book and in sight of home, the housewife reads: 'Caught by food enforcement officers in illegal possession of a ham. Go to prison for six months and forfeit all coupons.' I make a present of the idea to anybody who has sufficient enterprise and capital to develop it commercially.

NORTHERNER II

Leeds, 29th April, 1949

4

Hail the Housewives

Every scrap of rag, sheet of paper, ounce of berry, or sliver of soap was expected to go towards winning the war for Britain and aiding Britain's post-war recovery. Officially wastage was shunned while scrimping became a national obsession. Collection drives and recycling fanaticism jostled alongside those weary with having to make everything last. As time went on rationing became increasingly political as Labour stressed the necessity of keeping the ration while the Conservatives mobilised housewives in anti-rationing protest.

Lipstick

SIR – The 'filthy lipstick' of which a correspondent complains is for personal adornment and is every bit as important to the woman or girl who takes a pride in her general appearance as the one who takes a pride in her home. Actually I take great pride in both.

I for one wish the Government had the time to ration lipstick and powder, as then these commodities might be much easier to obtain. As a housewife who has been used to a large house and nine people to wash and clean for I consider the amount of soap and washing powder rationed per person is sufficient. Soda is unrationed and can be used for washing up and all cleaning purposes. I've always managed to keep my house perfectly clean and do all the personal and household washing with one bar of soap and one packet of washing powder per week, only lots of soda and elbow grease and plenty of disinfectants.

After all, how much better off we are than the women of other countries, if only we stop to consider, and how thankful we should be instead of always so much grumbling and complaining.

MRS D. PENGELLY

Plymouth, 19th February, 1942

Scrub Up

SIR – Our country must indeed be in a very bad way if the ridiculous soap ration is necessary. Have we a Minister of Health and any medical officers with practical knowledge of a household needs in the country? Are they aware that in any house there are, besides personal washing of the body, dishes to be washed, floors to be scrubbed, and, in thousands of cases, the household clothes to be washed weekly. Can any practical person say daily work of this kind could be done on this absurd soap ration?

If it is proceeded with in its present form a great increase of illness is bound to result. Heaven forbid this monstrous piece of folly should be allowed to stand. Housewives generally should be up in arms on this matter and insist on a reasonable ration.

It really does look as though more women are needed in Parliament. Why do not the Government stop the manufacture of filthy lipstick and nail varnish rubbish, which make the women of today look like Indian squaws? Personally, I have a home to keep going and clean, two men to wash for besides myself, including bed and table linen. I am by no means wasteful, but this ration is neither practical, healthy, nor clean. Such is our vaunted sanitation of today!

DISGUSTED HOUSEHOLDER

Plymouth, 12th February, 1942

Suds of Contempt

SIR – I read with increasing contempt the letter from 'Disgusted Householder'. We may be sure that the Government in the interest of public health would not have rationed soap unless in the interest of public safety it was absolutely necessary to do so. Indeed it is a source of satisfaction that such a step was not taken before. And, after all, is a cut of one-fifth such an overwhelming hardship. If one has learnt so very little from the course of events, such opinions are best not expressed in public.

DISGUSTED READER

Plymouth, 19th February, 1942

Soap Secondary

SIR – 'Disgusted Housewife' does not seem to realise yet this country is at war, fighting for its very existence, and that some of the essential fats and oils have to be brought across the seas at the cost of men's lives. Shipping space is required for armaments, and at present we are the best-fed nation in Europe. Does it matter what we are rationed if it is helping to win the war? 'Disgusted Housewife', I am afraid will be more disgusted before this war is ended.

T.E.H.

Plymouth, 19th February, 1942

Throw Me a Rope

SIR – The present world conflict is not only one of the battlefield, it is a war of production and raw materials. The country has responded magnificently to the call for salvage— indeed 12,000,000 homes are vital sources of raw materials. A further important step to obtain new raw materials is the Ministry of Supply Salvage of Waste Materials (No. 3) Order, which makes it an offence to destroy or throw away any rag, rope, or string, put rags, rope or string in a refuse bin or other receptacle used for domestic or trade refuse, or cause any rag, rope or string awaiting, or in the course of, collection or sale, to be or become mixed with any material or article other than rag, rope or string. A considerable extra tonnage of rags will thus become available for salvage—they are urgently needed to provide the raw materials for the production of numerous forms of equipment for the Fighting Forces.

I feel sure that everyone—housewives particularly—will respond to this Order in the spirit in which it has been made—the spirit to win the war; but I would like to take this opportunity through the columns of your papers, to appeal to them to release for salvage all the old worn-out, woollen, cotton and linen rages, pieces of carpets, sacking, rope and string, etc., that they can spare, not forgetting those old suits, frocks, underclothing, rugs and upholstery which can no longer serve their owners any useful purpose but can now render a valuable service to the Nation.

Rags should be kept as clean and dry as possible, separate from other salvage, ready for the collector. It is a good idea to keep a rag bag in which every odd bit of rag, rope and string can be kept for salvage; and, if possible, old floor-cloths and other dirty rags should be rinsed out and dried before putting those also in the rag bag.

J.S. MUGGLESTONE, BLACKWELL DISTRICT COUNCIL

Chesterfield, 17th July, 1942

Bones Assured

SIR – There is always a great cry for bones, so why not make it compulsory for butchers to bone all their meat? The bones could then be sent to the schools and the feeding centres, and after all the food value has been extracted the bones could be collected by the authorities.

SENSE

Cheltenham, 10th September, 1942

Herbaceous Heroes

SIR – The herb collecting season is here again, and doubtless many of your and their children will be collecting wild herbs to help meet the national need for these medicinal necessities. In some cases, organised parties of school children are already helping.

Last year, in some counties, no payment was made to collectors; the money was handed over to various charities. In others, either the individual collectors or the school and the bulk of the collectors are school children, sent their 'earnings' to a fund of their own selection, no fund benefiting to any great extent.

As Chairman of the Worcestershire County Herb Committee, I would like it to be known that we here feel that it would be a good thing if the collection of herbs should not be a commercial undertaking, but that the whole or part proceeds if the money given to collectors should go to endow a cot at the Hospital for Sick Children, Great Ormond Street, London. Rose hips are urgently needed to provide the valuable vitamin C. used in syrup for young children all over the country.

K.D. BRIGGS, W'RSHIRE COUNTY HERB COMMITTEE

Kirkcaldy, 2nd October, 1943

Clamour for Calico

SIR – Could not married women have, say, ten special marked household coupons to replace some of such things as towels, curtains, etc., or a permit for a certain number of yards of calico or such for sheets? We all want the war over, but feel we must have the few necessities.

EIGHT YEARS MARRIED

Hartlepool, 1st November, 1943

Bonfire of the Raggedy

SIR – Britain won the war. Who would think so? We are worse

off in every way (except that the bombing has ceased) than in the blackest days of the war. The rations are far too scanty and barely keep body and soul together, and, the increased ration for Christmas is a farce. Might be all right for big families, but for small households of two or three it is difficult. When we could buy spam it was a little help, but now we can't get it, and tins of meat cost 17 points, or almost a whole monthly ration.

As for clothes and household goods, words fail me! One of these days I shall have the biggest bonfire ever seen, and shall get rid of rags and patches, supposing I've to stay in bed until the next coupon issue! It's time we had a break. We are fast becoming like the Germans—all of us one pattern, everything arranged for us, even our thoughts!

Labour promised demobilisation. Thousands of our boys and girls are still under Government control and can't get home to jobs that are awaiting them.

'Annoying' Bevan had plenty to say about housing, but what is he doing about it now he is in power. Houses were to cost from £500 or £700 and last 10 years. The latest figures are £1250, &c. Why this increase? The Government are far too busy interfering in everybody else's business to get on with their own. We fought for freedom for every country but our own.

What if the housewives were to strike for more and better food and clothing, to say nothing of household goods?

If the Government applied some of their energy to produce these vital necessities at reasonable prices we might have something to be grateful for. There is too much talk of austerity. What we want is prosperity.

ONE OF MANY

Dundee, 27th November, 1945

Challenge to Cirencester

SIR – Congratulations to Cirencester for picking 4,667 lbs. rose-hips and to other Gloucestershire depots for putting their county at the head of the West of England. Rose-hips from this county are sent to the manufacturers of rose-hip syrup at Greenford, Middlesex, and we are assured by them that Hook Norton with a collection of 5,994 lbs, rose-hips averaging 43.21 lbs. per child, easily leads the London area. It appears that Hook Norton may well claim national rose-hip honours. If the collection is continued next year, Hook Norton throws out a friendly challenge to Cirencester to 'catch us if you can'.

ARTHUR G. MILLER, HOOK NORTON SCHOOL

Cheltenham, 14th December, 1945

Celebrating in Rags and Tatters

SIR – Coupons indeed. Surely the number 14 is a clerical error. There are unsold goods in plenty in the shops. Those goods are needed in our homes. Men objected to trousers without turn-ups. A cynical Board of Trade gives them the turn-ups without the trousers! But there is nothing funny in the ever-harassed housewives of Britain having to celebrate still more Victory days with rags and tatters for clothing, and rags and tatters past all mending. Forty coupons till September would be austere enough. Fourteen coupons will supply each housewife with handkerchiefs to dry tears of exasperated rage!

MARY MILLAR

Cheltenham, 21st February, 1946

Rations

SIR – At 4.15 p.m. on Saturday, after having got my week's rations for myself and child, I went into multiple stores. I put down my shopping bag to get something off one of the counters and, of course, had my eye off it for at least five minutes. Somebody else evidently hadn't, as when I went to pick it up it had disappeared. I don't suppose for one moment the person in question will be even sorry or will have the guts to return the goods, but I would like the opportunity of expressing what a mean and despicable type I think they are. While eating my rations I hope he or she gives a thought to the child who is going without to supply their greedy selves.

MRS J. BRETT

Lincoln, 30th April, 1946

Bedford's Menu Tips

SIR – My attention has been drawn to the statement made in Bedford recently by Mr. Skeffington-Lodge, M.P., that he eats one piece of bread only a day, and experiences difficulty in consuming it. I was surprised that an active man could maintain his energy on the present low rations without eating a considerable quantity of bread, and I decided to try it for myself. My day is taken up with my housework and shopping and the engagements and duties connected with the part I take in the local government of this borough. At the end of a week's trial I find that I cannot manage any longer on this reduced fare, and I think it would be of great help and interest to many of his constituents if the Member for Bedford would publish a sample week's menu. I find that his possible diet sheet is a topic of considerable interest and conjecture in the shopping queues in the town. I am of course, assuming that Mr. Skeffington-Lodge lives wholly on his rations, as most of us do, for his statement would be both stupid and beside the point if that were not the case.

DAPHNE JOYNSON

Bedford, 2nd August, 1946

Break Bread with the Enemy

SIR – I wish to protest at the way in which legitimate grievances of housewives are being exploited by party politicians under the guise of 'non-political' organisations. I attended the meeting, supposedly non-political in the Albert

Hall, Leeds. The audience was asked to support the abolition of bread rationing, to encourage their husbands not to work in their trade unions or ask for a 5-day week, and was told that the only way to make life easier would be to bring back Mr. Churchill and Lord Woolton. The meeting must have cost many pounds to organise, I calculate that at least £50 was spent on flowers alone.

DULLAPPLE

Leeds, 25th March, 1947

Housewives' Campaign

SIR – Mr Strachey, Minister of Food, descended this week on the housewives' stronghold at Dundee, but he didn't just chew them up as he expected. He seems to have been rather hard hit when he had to denounce in unmanly fashion: 'The middle-class ladies don't understand how the working-class ladies live.' Why should leaders of his type adopt such low tactics as trying to stir up one class against another, especially when the country is in such a mess?

In his interview he brought out the old nonsense. Never a straightforward promise to take all of Denmark's bacon or all the sugar the West Indies want to send us. He said also that only in the event of every country having a good wheat harvest would it be possible to do away with the B.U.'s, but he didn't say he would do it even then.

The latest cut in sausage meat takes away practically the only stand-by the housewives had left now that dried eggs have gone the same way as spam. To make up for the former, Mr Strachey is going to import one egg per head from Holland and another from Poland. Then he will dump them on the housewives' plate and say:—'Will you believe now that I am really trying to feed you?'

ONLOOKER

Dundee, 13th May, 1947

Where the Tractors Go

SIR – To-night the news came over the wireless that our bacon ration is again to be cut. At that precise moment I was reading an article in the South African *Cape Times*. It gives an illuminating account of how more than 3000 sheep were recently flown from England to Italy and Yugoslavia for breeding purposes, and 300 pedigree pigs from England to Yugoslavia. The planes used to take the sheep returned laden with cherries and raspberries.

Housewives, what do you think of it? We watched the abundant crop of raspberries in our gardens and countryside dropping to the ground for want of sugar to make them into our own good home-made jam. This same paper also tells how Switzerland has been supplied with tractors and bulldozers from Britain in order to complete her £4,000,000 airport with which Switzerland is hoping to attract the world tourist traffic. And yet our own farmers cannot get tractors to work our own land.

FARMER'S WIFE

Dundee, 13th October, 1947

Politicised Protest

SIR – So the Leeds housewives meeting was non-political! What nonsense! It was unmistakably an anti-government, anti-trade union, not to mention anti-husband propaganda meeting. Looking round, I saw what appeared to be a well-dressed, well-fed crowd, apparently not short of this world's goods.

ALICE JOLLY

Leeds, 25th March, 1947

The Housewife Vigilante

SIR – It seems that all critics of the Housewives' League are males. If the members of this association are not genuine housewives, then why do we not have letters in the newspapers from the genuine ones stating how satisfied they are with our present rations? The association members are but a small percentage the female population, so the genuine housewives must be in the majority.

AMUSED

Dundee, 26th November, 1947

The Anti-Housewife League

SIR – On taking the suggestions of Rather Amused, I would like to make a few observations. It has been said that if some part of body is not sufficiently exercised it eventually becomes useless. Here then the present-day rationing is a saviour of our brains.

Rationing brings into play part the brain that was never used by some housewives before. In its place money was used. In the days of not so long ago we housewives would stock our larders and, according to the means at our disposal, we would also build up reserve stock. If we became short of any commodity we then rifled this reserve stock and on our next shopping expedition augmented our supplies. It does not require much effort to take something out of a larder and then to replenish it.

Now we still have a reserve stock, but this stock not in our own larders. It is in the nation's larder, and when our rations are drawn from it, it someone's headache to refill it. But rest assured it is wisely and carefully guarded, much more so than it would be in an individual larder in a household. We can be sure of getting our weekly supply. Admittedly this is small, but with a little research this is where we can exercise our brain and cause the rations to become elastic. Where before we would discard odds and ends of food, we can now dish up these, disguised beyond recognition but still tasty and get quite a kick out of providing it.

Let us try to be content with what we have and quit moaning over what we have not. We were not meant to be spoon-fed, and if the luxuries of the past appear infrequently at our table we can appreciate them all the more when we do have them. To entertain a friend at every meal would not be so exciting as welcoming them occasionally. I would like to see an Anti-Housewives' League, a league those who are genuinely trying to make the best of things that get, leaving the Government to carry on with their job. I have yet to meet a walking skeleton advertising our supposed starvation diet, perhaps he stays home counting his daily intake of calories and prowling around for those which have escaped him.

MRS J. LEASK

Dundee, 1st December, 1947

Incessant Adolescent

SIR – The letter by Mrs Leask shows a very selfish attitude. I wonder if this lady knows anything about rationing. Has she ever tried to feed two or three teenagers on our present rations? Two pints of milk per week for a growing boy of twenty years doing a hard day's work! Many of the mothers of today are worn out trying to keep their grown-up families in good health. Mrs Leask may be well in with her grocer, butcher, and milkman so that rationing means nothing to her or else she may have sufficient cash to buy in the black market. But I would advise Mrs Leask just to take a walk along any of our main streets and study the faces of the people passing, especially the women folk. Never in our history have we been so poorly fed as we are today. Thanks to the muddling and extravagance of the present government Britain today is slowly becoming one of the poorest countries of the world.

A. M. W.

Dundee, 4th December, 1947

Enlarging Waistlines

SIR – Mrs Leask is unlikely to meet her walking skeleton, as bad balance of food and too much starch has had the opposite effect on most figures. A friend of mine (luckily slim) came over from America last summer, and in five weeks had put on 13 lbs. incidentally, no allowance is made for this, and the housewife a middle-age spread can only find utility garments and corsets meant for slim young girls!

And does she really think our brains are better used in eking out the fragments than in more useful items of work? The writer has had to say 'no more committees', however worthy the cause, as she simply cannot do more when so much time is wasted on the primitive hunt for food.

Another point, the townswoman, if she has money, can eat out, the countrywoman has to 'make do' for all meals.

And why store Empire sugar, not bought with dollars, when young and old are all in need of energy this winter?

COUNCILLOR

Dundee, 6th December, 1947

Suckling Adolescent

SIR – In reply to A. M. W., I would say her adjective 'selfish' is mischosen. I am not coveting her or anyone's rations. Is it selfish to use my own to the best advantage? Can she not supplement her teenage baby's milk with condensed or dried milk or does it not agree with his digestion?

I receive priority milk for my two children as they are both under five, so obviously this milk is not labelled black market. Perhaps it is selfish for mothers to accept this milk when A. M. W.'s 20-year-old is still on the bottle. The nature of my husband's work is such that I cannot go out unless some kind friend offers to stay in the house so I cannot take a survey of faces as suggested. Nor can I stand in queues.

My personal affairs can be of no interest, but if I explain briefly that we started in business this year (not a food business, please note) without any capital after a long spell of unemployment, perhaps this will suffice to prove that I have no dealings with a black market and my retailers are honest men.

Regarding the corsets for Councillor's friend, perhaps her meandering around the ships will reduce her figure and therefor dispense with the need for them. I hope so. If Councillor has less committees to attend she will have time to think more and talk less, which, I am sure, will be her family's advantage.

Finally, I can write from experience of both town and country living and making do.

MRS J. LEASK

Dundee, 7th December, 1947

Housewives and Mr Strachey

SIR – May I be permitted to thank the loyal housewives from near and far who rallied round on Saturday afternoon and helped to make the meeting with Minister of Food Mr Strachey a success. Although Mr Strachey failed to answer one single question, I believe we may hope that our plea for the undernourished adolescent will bring some result. If so, we shall not have endured in vain the tumult and the shouting of those who sought to play into Mr Strachey's hands.

I do not think Mr Strachey went away feeling that he had had a half-holiday. He certainly could not call us 'mild as milk' this time. Virulent as vitriol was more like it.

LORNA TAYLOR, SCOTTISH HOUSEWIVES' ASS.

Dundee, 2nd February, 1948

Bare Cupboards

SIR – We learn with astonishment that 'housewives are over-stocking,' that 'every housewife to-day has a cupboard she would've been proud to have four or five years ago!' Thus said Sir W. Darling in the House of Commons on Monday night. As this gentleman is an Edinburgh draper, he must be aware how little one can buy with four coupons a month and how much we now lack after seven years of clothing coupons.

On what facts does Sir William base this statement? Presumably he was referring to our store and linen cupboards as well as to our wardrobes. Any housewife will testify that, even in well-run Scottish homes, the food cupboards are practically empty, that hospitality is now almost unknown and that we cannot teach the rising generation to bake and cook in our own kitchens.

We as a nation are worse fed than at any time within living memory. We are not achieving the production targets because our people are not now fed and clad to sustain life and do a decent day's work in the vagaries of our climate.

This is a fact which the Minister of Food, Mr Strachey, still refuses to face.

On March 16 last Mr Strachey received a deputation from the Dundee Housewives' Association. He admitted that the shops were stocked with points goods which we are unable to buy with 28 points per month, and that some of the food is now deteriorating. He was shown a tin of meat which was part of a consignment declared by the city analyst to be unfit for human consumption and dated February 1942! Asked about the sugar situation he stated, 'We have a fair amount of sugar. We have about five months' supply always in the country,' yet once more for jam-making we are asked to make do with a meagre one pound per ration book perhaps, as usual.

Sir William must know that, far from achieving the new look (sic), most women are now clad 'in unwomanly rags,' that for long enough we have even been patching patches, that our curtains resemble nothing so much as the tattered banners in his own St Giles, that soap is in very short supply, and that most housewives are at their wits' end to find a change of bed and body linen and also towels.

Well, well! 'Knowledge comes, but wisdom lingers.' Sir William would do well to return home and let the winds of the North clear his vision. Let him leave our myopic rulers to muddle along. In London the misogynist Cripps has been given complete dictatorial powers over all of us. That is understandable. 'In the country of the blind the one-eyed man is king.' To Scotswomen, however, the defection of the gallant Sir William is harder to bear.

MRS M.S. CLARK, DUNDEE HOUSEWIVES' ASS.

Dundee, 22nd April 1948

Dollars or Food?

SIR – Replying to Major Poole's assertion that at meetings held by the Lichfield Housewives' Association truth is jettisoned in the interests of political propaganda, we would ask whether this charge also applies to *The Times* and the *Spectator*, which state: 'It is not now world scarcity (of food) which is the main source of Britain's difficulties but her own need to conserve dollars' *Times*, December 14th. 'During 1948 stocks of cereals and linseed-oil have been accumulating in Argentine ports, and underground silos are now being constructed for the storing of two million tons of the next wheat crop ... abundant harvests have been gathered in the northern hemisphere; and even tropical countries such as Brazil have increased their cultivation of grain' *Spectator* December 17th. This Association understands the necessity for conserving dollar, but, with 'The Times' asks: 'How much could these difficulties be diminished by different methods of buying'. Finally we would point out that Belgium and Poland, both of whom were over-run during the war, are to abolish food rationing completely as from January 1st next.

MRS C. STAIT-GARDNER, LICHFIELD HOUSEWIVES' ASS.

Lichfield, 24th December, 1948

We Get Enough to Eat

SIR – With reference to the recent annual meeting of the Conservative Women's Organisation in London, as a mere male I am not entitled to say much about food but I think that everyone who is fair, who knows how to use food, and who is not prejudiced against the Government, will readily admit that we are getting enough to eat—perhaps not all the things we would like to have, but we do get enough, and are we not better off than the Continental countries who are off the ration and whose working-class people cannot afford to buy some of the things which are cheap, though rationed, in this country?

Statistics show that on the whole the nation is healthier. Look at the picture on the front page showing pupils of the Naunton Park School at lunch in their new canteen. Has anyone ever seen such a bunch of healthy, round-faced and straight-legged children in one group? On another page of the same paper is a report of an American woman who gained six pounds in weight during a short working holiday in England.

C. J. WOODHOUSE, F. R.A.F.

Cheltenham, 26th May, 1949

In a Pickle

SIR – The 'fair shares' fairy tale is worked out: also the jibing references to 'the rich'. Most women know the extent of Socialist 'benefits' by this time; these are less bread, meat, sugar, tea, fats, petrol, beat and light all dearer too, than at any time in the 30 years before the war. Then, all these were available to all at cheap prices; and though we know some foods are short, yet bulk buying makes them both scarce and dear.

And now the Chancellor Sir Stafford Cripps has the impudence to ask for more savings, though we are taxed to death and most of our capital has had to be used in order to live. Surely the man must be wilfully blinded by his association with the rest of our crazy Government, who now shiver in the cold blast of public disgust.

As a relative cotton mill owner wrote to me yesterday, 'I'm glad the beggars are going on; let them finish in the mess they have made'. Sir Stafford Cripps denied devaluation time and time again, yet he devalued. Socialist negatives should be taken as a warning of things to come, and the words 'we have no intention' are like Socialist promises—meant to broken.

J. BRUNDRETT BICKLE,

Taunton, 29th October, 1949

Strive Wives!

SIR – In reply to the letter 'War Widow' I say good luck to any housewife whatever her nationality who justifiably complains about our food rationing, and if the British housewives were not so complacent about it all I, for one, am certain we should not be in this awful position we are to-day. The women of this country could have done something about it and still can. So housewives, let's have some action, refuse to buy.

A BRITISH HOUSEWIFE

Portsmouth, 12th December, 1950

5

Restaurant Roast

Hotels and restaurants provided opportunities for those with the means to 'eat off the ration'. Hotel guests could get three meals provided for them as well as the opportunity to gorge on rations in their rooms. Restaurants also initially offered an oasis of freedom in a tough food regime. However, in 1942 it was stipulated that meals in hotels and restaurants could not charge over 5 shillings per customer. The meals served could not be more than three courses; and at most only one course could contain either meat, fish or poultry. Nevertheless luxury hotels and restaurants could still exceed these price limitations sparking fury at those perceived to be gaming the rationing system.

Entertainment in war time Britain was changing and much debate raged about the morality of cinemas opening on Sunday and the potentially satanic influence of jazz. While some turned to God in the war other sought comfort in films.

Movie Moralising

SIR – Men say: 'Give the troops light music and coarse jokes all the time, we must keep their minds off all this religious stuff' Poor ignorance indeed! Let me say this: the troops in all places need their hallowed Sunday. Why should there be antagonism about the keeping of the Sabbath? It should be kept, with one mind, by all people as being the performing of one of the distinct commands of God.

C. R. MEPHAM

Hastings and St Leonards, 17th February, 1940

Cinema Suffering

SIR – I was particularly interested in a letter signed A. E. Meurisse, who is obviously very much against the opening of Sunday cinemas. Now I wonder, has this lady ever been in the positon of a domestic servant in a town like Hastings where she perhaps has no friends and no home; where she has a comfortless kitchen and a cold bedroom as an alternative to her Sunday out. Even supposing her kitchen were comfortable and her bedroom warm and cosy – every girl wishes to be away from their employers for a little time once or twice a week if she is normal. I wonder if A. E. Meurisse has ever had to walk wet, cold streets to kill time on a Sunday evening to get a break from pots and pans, gas stoves and sinks, and the eternal supervision of the employer?

The anti-Sunday cinema crowd will at once say: 'Churches are open to those that wish to visit them'. I have known the utter wretchedness of a Sunday afternoon off in the winter-time. I became a regular church-goer in a parish here for nearly two years. I enjoyed the services very much but no one made me welcome to the church's social circles. I became aware of snobbishness and coldness, although I have no doubt if I had been a daughter of a local prosperous tradesman instead of someone's little general help, my company would have been sought by the vicar and his wardens.

I truly believe in God, but I am convinced He would far rather people like us could pay a shilling and have a rest and warmth and the simple entertainment of the pictures.

ONE WHO HAS SUFFERED

Hastings and St Leonards, 17th February, 1940

Laggards in Hotels

SIR – May I beg a few inches of your paper to express my disgust at the indifferent way in which hotel residents decline to help with war-time sacrifices? I have a hotel accommodating 40 guests. Not one has offered to fire-watch, in response to my appeals, and more than 50 per cent endeavour in every way possible to induce the waitresses to give them rations to which they are not entitled. It is a pity that these people, who receive many advantages over private householders, do everything they can to make things difficult.

PROPRIETOR

Cheltenham, 15th March, 1941

In Defence of Hotel Laggards

SIR – With reference to the controversy over hotel fire-watching and rationing, I should like to say that in the first instance I have a most willing helper in one of my residents and all my male staff, and I feel sure that any other visitor or member of the staff would be quite willing to help in an emergency. In regard to the second point, both my visitors and staff accept the rationing laws in a most patriotic manner.

G. MEADMORE, MANAGERESS

Cheltenham, 21st March 1941

Guests' Evasion

SIR – Permit me to enter the arena in the laggard controversy. I am a daily maid in an hotel in this town. The guests do evade their responsibility of fire-watching. They go to bed or pretend to forget. They have all the things we cannot get from the shops, because things are saved for hotels, such as rabbits, tripe, sausage, jam, marmalade, honey, dates, figs, prunes, currants, sultanas, eggs, biscuits, tins of beef, and plenty of cheese. The guests do try to get more than their allowance. Having had a full breakfast, a three-course lunch, tea and full dinner, they visit the shops and bring in more food, which they consume in their rooms. On many occasions a maid has eight people in bed for breakfast and lunch, after which they get up and play bridge or go out.

I suggest that the laggards expect the maids to go on the roof after running up and down stairs carrying things to them all day.

P.S. I am over 40 and too old for war work.

GLADIATOR

Cheltenham, 21st March, 1941

Look Out of Luck

SIR – I have found my staff very wiling, and the guests have volunteered to help because they realise how hard the staff have to work during the day. Rationing is bound to cause complaints, but I have found these few and far between, and the more patriotic ones have usually downed the so-called 'extra ration wranglers'.

HOTEL IRVING

Cheltenham, 21st March, 1941

Moral Flashback

SIR – Once again God's command is ignored, and now theatres and music-halls are to be opened on Sunday. This fact was received with cheers in the House of Commons.

Was there ever a time in the history of man when so much time was given to soldiers for amusement? Those who have listened to the programmes provided for the Forces for six days a week must know that so much of it is neither morally uplifting nor helpful. It is an insult to our brave men that they must get that kind of thing on Sundays, too.

God is ready to give us victory. Are we ready for it?

J. B. C

Cheltenham, 21st March, 1941

Self-Serving

SIR – Whilst some people were able to secure extra rations every day through canteens or cafes others through lack of opportunity could not do so. Surely this is not fair. There are also many others who are unable to afford meals out, yet could manage a shilling or two more for extra rations for home consumption. It is in respect of these two classes of people that the rationing scheme fails in its profession of equality for all.

HYSON GREEN

Nottingham, 26th June, 1941

Dysfunctional Dining

SIR – The rationing of food, and in particular of bread, is uppermost in people's minds to-day. As a recently-released soldier, home after an absence of four years, I am amazed by circumstances which, to my mind, make the system of rationing a complete farce.

Walking from St. John's Station along the High Street to Bunyan Statue, one passes no fewer than twelve establishments serving meals without so much as a mention of surrendering a coupon or a 'point.' Here, then, is a situation where, with sufficient money, one may eat throughout the week and, at the weekend, obtain with a ration-book food for seven days. Surely this system is wrong and defeats the whole object of rationing.

Could not a system be devised whereby one's ration-book was marked in some way every time a meal was consumed in a hotel or restaurant? As the Ministry of Food seem capable of devising sundry schemes of control, surely this would not be beyond their powers.

ATHOS

Bedford, 12th July, 1946

Dining Discord

SIR – I agree with every word in the letter condemning the system by which people who can afford it may supplement their rations by feeding at restaurants and hotels. Having been abroad the last ten years and in many countries, I find that most of the shops are full of food, but it takes money to buy it and it is the working people who suffer every time. Our rationing system defeats its own object.

Ex-N.C.O.

Bedford, 12th July 1946

Tell the Caterers

SIR – Why all this palaver between the hotelkeepers and the Ministry of Food? Simply say that their allocation is to be reduced by a certain amount, and end the matter. The everyday housewife, I am certain, will not have the opportunity of any discussion when the next cut in her basic rations is impending.

EQUALITY

Leeds, 25th August, 1947

Official Hotel Hypocrisy

SIR – With regard to your report on the Kirkburton food prosecution, presumably the visits to the hotel referred to were considered an essential preliminary to providing evidence for the case and were made in the public interest. To remove any doubt, it would be interesting to know what proportion of the £8 14s. involved in 20 meals consumed by the Food Ministry official, his wife and daughter and two supernumeraries from the Ministry will be regarded as a charge against public funds and whether there is any question of incidental expenses for the time so nobly sacrificed by these people on behalf of their short-rationed fellowmen.

JUST THE JOB!

Leeds, 12th March, 1948

Lodgers' Rations

SIR – At two out of three lodgings in Leeds, I have had my ration book overdrawn. In the last instance I took lodgings for a few days only, as the landlady had a booking to follow. She took my ration book, and instead of getting an emergency card, re-registered me with all her tradesmen. On leaving, after 12 days, I found she had used 20 points from Period 2, instead of an entitlement of 12, two months' preserves, one moth's tea, and six points from Period 3, which had not then started. The Food Office informs me that there is no redress against this kind of thing; ration books are holders' own responsibility.

TWICE BITTEN

Leeds, 17th September, 1948

Cheesed Off

SIR – I am a rural worker in the building trade and recently applied for the usual extra ration of cheese which has been granted for the past years. But on the last period of application, to my surprise I was informed that I was no longer eligible while working in an area of two miles from any licensed house, café or catering establishment.

Dinnertime in the winter period is only half an hour. Is it possible to go two miles in that period, also to spend 3s in getting a portion of bread and cheese—the like of which, if I had the cheese ration, would cost eight-pence?

WALL

Lichfield, 24th December, 1948

6

Poisonous Pleasures

Neither tobacco nor alcohol were rationed during the war as the government feared rationing would fuel an already overheated black-market. Debate raged around these narcotics which were seen as both essential, and hazardous, to the war effort. Puritanical prohibitionists flirted with temperance whereas others fiercely defended what they saw as their last indulgences in the war.

Cigarettes and Biscuits

SIR – There is still a lot of argument about rationing of cigarettes. In spite of repeated appeals to smokers there will always be that despicable minority who go from queue to queue to grab as much and as often as possible.

Last Saturday I stood in a queue for over an hour after walking four miles with a pram, and was very disgusted to hear a man boasting to another person that both he and his wife (who was with him) had each got 40 cigarettes from the same store on the previous day, also 20 from another shop, and yet a further 20 of a well-known brand from another shop, and they each had 40 more from this store then, making a total of 200 in two days, with how many more would they get before going home. They had also been in a biscuit queue, and each had 1 lb of biscuits.

What do two elderly people want with 2 lb of biscuits when

there are hundreds of poor kiddies who never see one from one month's end to another because their parents are much too busy to trot around from queue to queue?

Rationing is the only way to stop this disgusting habit.

SHARE-ALIKE

Cheltenham, 4th August, 1941

240 Million Pounds

SIR – Tobacco Controller Alexander Maxwell stated that Britain smoked 240,000,000 pounds of leaf in 1941. That 50,000 men and women work in tobacco factories, and that the flow of leaf continues to be eight per cent above that before the war. This enormous amount is carried in our ships in order that a proportion the population can indulge in the silly and quite unnecessary habit of drawing smoke into their mouths and blowing it out again.

It is to be a comfort. What about the comfort of folk such as I, who detest it? Non-smoking railway carriages are usually invaded by smokers. I have given up going to the cinema owing to the necessity of changing my seat so many times to avoid someone's filthy tobacco smoke. Even in restaurants tobacco smoke usually wafts across one's face; I have observed women are the greatest offenders in this respect. I would like to see cigarettes rationed to ten per week and tobacco finally prohibited altogether. The loss in revenue could be raised from income-tax. I would pay more income tax to live in a tobaccoless country.

F. SMITH, SUPPLY CHIEF PETTY OFFICER

Cheltenham, 4th August, 1941

Silly Smoking

SIR – I am so sorry for poor Supply C.P.O Smith that he has to suffer so much from pollution by tobacco smoke. There are millions of 'silly' people with this 'silly' habit including very famous and intellectual men. C.P.O. Smith is a bigot.

I happen to be a woman and a smoker, so I am a great offender in his eye. Women are doing a man's job and often facing danger, and during some anxious moments have found that 'obnoxious' weed a consolation. There is a great (not silly-minded) gentleman who smokes a cigar. It would be interesting to know whether it is a help or a hindrance during these momentous days.

Poor C.P.O Smith has had to stay away from the cinema and the restaurant? So may I suggest he finds another planet to live on, as there can't be any corners left on our silly world, where the fumes can't be smelled. I wouldn't go with him. I would rather remain and be yours.

A SILLY SMOKER

Portsmouth, 15th August, 1942

Facts

SIR – The following are facts (1) necessity; tobacco is a dangerous vegetable growth with narcotic properties from its nicotine and pyridine bodies. (2) Reduction in import: Three ounces of sugar imported would do the nation and all smokers a thousand times more good than the three ounces of tobacco. There are some arguments for sacrifice for cargo space for munitions and necessities by one who has been a smoker for 46 years.

SACRIFICE

Portsmouth, 15th August, 1942

Smoke of War

SIR – A nice letter, Mr Non Smoker, but one I fail to agree with. You and other non-smokers have the right, when travelling in non-smoking carriages to stop those who disregard the notice. That should rid you of one of your troubles. The other, the cinema, you have chosen the best way.

Sorry if I am being rude, but cannot help it after reading your letter. I'm going back off leave, to a lonely spot in the country, where I and many more see very few cinemas and thank our lucky stars we are able to get smokes because we enjoy them. You should try it.

SOLDIER

Portsmouth, 15th August, 1942

Finest Chap in Blighty

SIR – Spare me a small space in reply to Bentley 4½. Like him, I am a lifelong non-smoker and total abstainer, but I am not of his opinion. He would like to ban all tobacco, and rob the men who are fighting hard for all of us. He is definitely wrong when he says there is no comfort in a cigarette. In the last Great War it was my privilege to visit a military hospital somewhere on the South Coast. One Sunday afternoon I arrived there just after a party of wounded. I was admitted to the ward at once. After having a few words with them, I asked if they would like a few cigarettes or chocolate, and with one voice they all said: 'God bless you, Captain. Give us a few cigarettes; you are the finest chap we have seen since we arrived in Blighty'.

I pass this on to Bentley 4½. I agree that smoking should be rationed because it would be better for all.

CURLY

Portsmouth, 15th August, 1942

My Lady Nicotine

SIR – May I congratulate your correspondent 'Sacrifice' on being that *rara avis*, a smoker who realises that tobacco is a non-essential that could be replaced by imports vital to the wellbeing of all? He is the exception that proves the rule, or rather two rules which would always prevent me becoming a smoker.

In the first place, smoking appears to make otherwise pleasant and companionable people abominably selfish. They expect to be allowed to enjoy their tobacco, often in an atmosphere that could almost be cut with a knife. That's all right. I've no wish to dictate to others what form their pleasure shall take, but I do expect them to extend the same tolerance to me.

The second, and I think worse, effect of smoking appears to be a complete lack of self control. Once a person starts smoking, he or she must have that cigarette or pipe regardless of consequences, and if for any reasons they are deprived of it, become sulky or bad tempered. As we have rationing of almost every essential, and I think most of us suffer cheerfully, tobacco should be rationed also.

However, I haven't much hope. Tobacco makes a big contribution to the revenue, and those in authority are no doubt as reluctant as the man in the street to abandon My Lady Nicotine.

FREEDOM

Portsmouth, 17th August, 1942

Smoking Chairs

SIR – 'Sacrifice' is lucky to get a half column of your valuable space to tell us that immoderate smoking is harmful, but he is not so tiresome as others who have written to little purpose save, perhaps, to suggest that they;

Compound for sins they are inclined to

— By Damming those they have no mind to.

— Deprive smokers of tobacco, and they find another, and perhaps even more noxious weed, J. M. Barrie, you will remember told how his friend Jimmy Moggridge smoked a cane chair; it is true it was at school, but it just shows what might happen.

V. E. G. CHURCHER

Portsmouth, 17th August, 1942

A Parting Shot

SIR – As the originator of the discussion on tobacco and shipping space, allow me to thank all, especially C.P.O.

Smith and 'Sacrifice' whose concise and relevant letters of support were refreshing to read. The outstanding fact has emerged that our import of tobacco last year amounted to 240,000,000 lbs. equal in weight to more than 5,000 20-ton tanks.

P.W. informs me that tobacco is necessary to maintain morale. I realise that we live in an age of false values as witness the statement from one writer that '95 per cent of the men of the R.N. and M.N. would risk their lives for a grasp of that fragrant weed' but never did I believe that in the midst of a life-and-death struggle I should live to see narcotics described—as necessities, demanding priority over war supplies, when our shipping losses are giving grave anxiety. These nicotine addicts must wonder how on earth their ancestors managed to survive the past six thousand years without it. The Spartan, to give but one example, had very little the matter with their morale and for that matter neither had King Alfred, Richard I or Robin Hood. And what of the classic example of unshakable morale the bravery of the Christian slaves under Nero? They knew the secret of morale, if it can be called a secret. Surely our enemies would rejoice, were it really true that the average Briton's morale required boosting twenty times a day.

Is it too much to ask smokers to ration themselves to half, at any rate their present consumption, and thus free the ships for 2500 20-ton tanks, or if not tanks, 50,000 tons of alternative war supplies such as machinery, for which the demand here is colossal? Ludendorff attributed Germany's defeat in the last war to the failure of the potato crop in 1917. Never let it be said that the fate of the world hangs upon the tobacco crop in 1942.

BENTLEY 4½

Portsmouth, 17th August, 1942

The Price of Abstinence

SIR – I noticed from your issue of the 10th that, among other reasons, the National British Women's Total Abstinence Union opposed the renewal of the White Rock Pavilion because of the 'Keep-fit' campaign. This is a misleading suggestion. The fitness campaign does not take any stand against moderate drinking, and alcoholic refreshments are served at some of its social functions.

Another equally misleading excuse for their opposition was given as war-time need for the economy. If the consumption of alcoholic drinks was cut down or completely alienated it is very unlikely that any money now so spent would find its way into more useful channels. The alternatives to the popular alcoholic drinks which are mainly favoured by the home public are brewed and distilled in this country, are results of English and Scottish labour of, to a great extent, home-grown grain and sugar, and their sale provides the National Exchequer with about £100,000,000 each year through direct liquor taxation only. A healthy sum towards our huge war outlay. On the other hand, the probable alternatives, popular teetotal drinks are practically all imported, are the results of foreign labour from foreign-grown produce and they pay little to the National Exchequer.

Putting on one side the fact that any curtailment of drinking facilities is against the wishes of the majority of the general public, it is false wartime economy.

R. G. FIFE

Hastings and St Leonards, 17th February, 1940

Rationing of Beer

SIR – Since Lord Woolton's (Minister of Food) statement on the above subject was published (and before) there has been much comment from the teetotallers on the unfairness of the lack of action. Let it be clearly understood that the majority of drinkers will put up with rationing, if and when the time comes for it. What they are against is the foisting on the country, by the teetotal minority, prohibition in the guise of a war-time necessity. Temporary rationing is one thing, whilst a prohibition law is another. We can all remember the restrictions entered on the Statute Book during the last war, and we know how many of them are still with us.

Another point is this: If the authorities can get a more wholehearted interest in the war effort by allowing the retention of a minor luxury, and one which is largely home-produced, it appears good business to me to let it be that way. It isn't as if the food available would be greatly increased by a cessation of brewing.

M. G. HUNT

Aylesbury, 29th May, 1942

Liquor Rationing

SIR – As a member of the Mothers' Union may I say how deeply we feel on this question of strong liquor as regards the troops, especially those from overseas. We do not wish to be hard on them, but now and again one hears how some overstep the mark, with tragic results. What a lot of trouble and careless talk could be prevented if only they were rationed the same as we are in the things most necessary to our well-being. We feel for their womenfolk, who undoubtedly think them in good hands while over here, until the time when they will meet again. So therefore it is up to us to do all we can for them, even in this direction, of preventing them getting into trouble and overstepping the mark. And that is where the welcomed cup of tea comes in, which, given in the right spirit, does far more good than all the liquor in the world.

MRS E. COLLINS

Lewes, 26th February, 1943

Enough with the Clubs and Pubs

SIR – Both clubs and pubs seem inseparable from the major question of entertainment. We already have a vast display of licensed houses and many clubs, which makes it apparent that we need not ask for more.

It seems to me that some suitable medallion, in honour of those who gave their lives so freely, should be given to the nearest of kin, or there should be a cash gift if they are in need, as a token of our respect and mourning.

Clubs and pubs are not merely 'entertainment' but often a costly luxury, diverting men from the best club of all—the home.

When one observes how much liquor and tobacco are consumed, it is clear that no added facilities are advisable in this direction.

PROUD MOURNER

Cheltenham, 20th March, 1946

Christmas Bottleneck

SIR – I should be grateful for the renewed help of your paper in inviting readers to assist in averting, or at least lessening, the acute shortage in retail supplies of bottled beer, wines and spirits that must occur at Christmas unless, from now on, empty bottles are promptly returned, complete with stopper, to the off-licence or other premises.

The bottle shortage to-day is unprecedented and is getting worse. Failure on the part of the public to co-operate with the retail distributors may well mean a dry Christmas for many who otherwise might get something.

R. GEO, FEDERATION OF OFF-LICENCE HOLDERS

Hartlepool, 19th October, 1946

Why Didn't Somebody Think of the Housewives?

SIR – Housewives are again the sufferers under the latest impositions of our present rulers. Imagine increasing the cost of essentials of our very meagre diet and at the same time having the temerity to reduce the price of beer! It is time the women of Britain took strong action and saw to it that their representatives on local councils, county councils and in

Parliament really voiced the claims of the housewives, the most down-trodden and self-sacrificing section of the community.

How can a government expect better exports and greater output on less rations? Those rations which are permitted are at prices which the working and middle classes can ill afford.

RAY WARD BATESON

Leeds, 8th February, 1949

7

Curdled Milk

Milk was one the trickier items to ration as it quickly went off and had to be supplied near the source. Milk gripes raged around the insufficient amount of milk given for tea, alleged disgraceful milk wastage at schools, and a battle for surplus milk between the elderly and young. Dried milk and cream became an ersatz for fresh milk. 'Household Milk' was dried skimmed milk and meant to replace fresh milk. 'National Dried Milk' was a dried 'full cream' milk powder and meant to feed infants.

Cheese production soon ground to a halt and government mandates to produce a strictly regulated bland 'Government Cheddar' set the cheese industry back for years. Butter meanwhile was replaced with margarine much to traditionalists chagrin.

Cheese on Rails

SIR – It has been announced that agricultural workers are to receive a special cheese ration. Why these workers, who have regular daily hours of work, and a fixed time to be home for a hot meal, while hundreds of railwaymen, like myself, sign on duty all hours of the day and night for eight hours, which often extends to 10, 12 and up to 14 hours (owing to the pressure of war traffic), find it a great difficulty what to pack up for the period of hours to be worked? Why not a little more cheese or even a portion of corn-beef for this purpose?

H. ROSE

Lincoln, 25th March, 1941

Mouse Trap

SIR – It had been broadcast with éclat: it arrived as a small slice, about the volume of a cake of toilet soap.

There were five of us. We looked at it wistfully. A single invalid could have consumed it during the week with ease.

We had to decide what to do with it, to avoid contention. Now we were visited daily by our neighbour's cat, so we determined to bribe him with daily snippets of cheese to catch the mice which troubled us.

But he, being a well-fed and highly-respectable cat, merely sniffed at our bribe and turned it away. We felt humiliated. However, we revived when Aunt Ermintrude suggested we should use the snippet to bait a mousetrap. So Jane hurried off and bought a sudden-death trap. But the cheese remained unassailed by mice for three days, then dried, cracked, and fell off the hook. Fortunately, we had preserved the rest of the precious slice under a moist compress in the pantry, so we baited the trap once more. Alas, after another three blank days, we could no longer maintain, with James, that the mice had passed the bait by because of its rarity in war-time—for it was perfectly obvious—crushing conclusion—that even our mice despised our cheese ration.

GOURMET

Cheltenham, 22nd May, 1941

Milk for the Elderly

SIR –I was very pleased to see in the *Echo* that someone is taking up the matter of milk for the aged.

It is time something was done, especially where there is one person living alone, and one has to give up eight points for a tin of milk, which does not leave many for other things.

WELL-WISHER

Cheltenham, 16th December 1942

Milk Grousers

SIR – The new system of distributing milk is causing great concern among the public. Previous to the new arrangements many people were receiving a greater supply of milk than what they were entitled to.

On Sunday, February 7, the new system of milk delivery came into force and myself and other dairymen were to supply many strangers with milk. The dairyman's quota remains the same and his new round has been calculated in a rational so that he should not require extra milk. But, as mentioned before, the public are constantly reminding their new dairyman as to the quantity they were previously receiving. This in itself is keeping the dairyman behind in his deliveries, the reason being that he has to explain to each of these grousers that milk is rationed and that he also is rationed.

Somehow the public think that there is a difference between ordinary rationing and milk rationing. Would a person go to his or her grocer's and say 'I want more butter, etc., because what I am at present receiving is insufficient?' No, they understand that butter, etc., is rationed, and that they cannot get more than that which they are due to. Here there is the difference to which I refer. The public are saying: 'I want more milk.'

May I respectfully ask the public to realize that milk is rationed, and has been rationed for quite a while.

DAIRYMAN

Sunderland, 12th February, 1943

Milk Malady

SIR –Things are fast coming to the ridiculous when people

with sick notes cannot get milk and those without can have milk. The reason, it seems is this: pay the day before the week's money is due and the milk is there next morning. People who have paid cannot be left without!

BE HUMAN

Leeds, 21st March, 1943

Equal Advantage

SIR – I am a soldier's wife with one child, aged nine. My Army allowance is £2 7s 6d. My child has a blue ration book and I have to pay 4d per pint for milk. A neighbour, whose husband is in a good steady job earning £6 to £7, has one child, same age, with a green ration book. She gets her milk from the same man at 2d per pint.

Can anyone tell me how I can get equal advantage with my more fortunate neighbour? My milkman says it is not fair, but he can't do anything.

SOLDIER'S WIFE

Dundee, 31st August, 1944

Milk Farce

SIR – I also cannot understand the milk rationing. While my family have only their two pints, others nearby have double and treble the amount delivered daily.

If some farmers have so much surplus, surely this ought to be pooled, so that there can be a more even distribution. Rationing of milk at the present moment is a farce, and should be seen into. Where should we have been if all rationing had been so abused?

Many housewives feel very strongly on this point, and it is time the authorities ceased being so blind as to what is going on all around them.

ALSO CURIOUS

Cheltenham, 16th November, 1944

Something Should Be Done

SIR – I fully endorse all that 'Also Curious' says regarding so many people having more than enough milk, and others—like myself, on my own—not having sufficient. What is the cause of this unfairness?

Over the week-end I was very unwell with a sore throat and heavy cold, and had to use my precious drop of milk for a cup of tea during Saturday night, in consequence of which I had no milk to use on Sunday. The milk-man does not deliver to me on Sundays.

Although very unwell, I had to turn out in the raid to find a café for a pot of tea, for which I was charged sixpence: in fact, the small meal cost three shillings and threepence.

We are told to keep healthy and to save, but, I ask, how?

Most of us do not mind going without things, if we have to do so, but when we see others with so much milk it makes us wonder.

UNFAIR PLAY

Cheltenham, 16th November, 1944

Alice in Milkland

SIR – The letter referring to the wastage of milk should surely help to stir public apathy into some action against this scandal of officialdom. Instances given by your correspondent are not singular.

Surplus milk, according to the judgement of officials must be refused to human beings, but may be given to pigs or thrown down the drain and further, a man who sells his surplus milk to the old or sick must be prosecuted for this kindly action! This is officialdom run mad.

If milk rationing is still necessary, and the simple way of allowing a milkman to sell his surplus milk must not be allowed, could not there be receiving centres for any surplus where allocations might be made to those in need who might be instructed to being a certified guarantee.

Cannot the local MPs persuade the Ministry of Food to cut

this irrational and most wasteful red tape and let people who need it have the benefit of all available milk.

LADY MARY R. MUNDAY

Plymouth, 18th August, 1945

Milk Puddle

SIR – Many of us would be obliged if the milk position could be made clear. In some parts of town people can get as much milk as they like and when they like (especially if they are tradesmen), while others never get more than three pints a week.

The point is; are we rationed or are we not? Rationing was brought into being to make things fair to all not to give extras to the few. Yet many of us cannot enjoy a milk pudding unless we give up our tea milk. For the elderly and old this is a very great blow.

PUZZLED

Bedford, 7th June, 1946

Gone to the Dogs

SIR – It seems to be a common practice in this town for milk distributors to leave crates of milk bottles, full or empty, on the ground at convenient places for distribution. This exposes the crates and the bottles to contamination by dogs, as well as by dust, etc. I have personally seen crates of full bottles which have obviously been defiled by dogs in this way.

Some distributors place crates of full bottles on top of crates of empty bottles, which protects the full bottles from the attentions of at least the smaller dogs. But it does not seem desirable that even empty crates or bottle should be defiled in this way.

Cannot distributors do better than this? Is our health authority interested?

RESIDENT

Bedford, 2nd August, 1946

Miffed at Milk

SIR – Your correspondent 'Utterly Disgusted' inquires how she can feed her family properly on the milk ration. Admittedly it takes a bit of doing, but hasn't she heard of tinned milk and the household milk

I, too, am very sore about the half-pint, as I live alone, but have used tinned milk ever since I have not been able to get cream, which I always used to have when obtainable. The household milk is very nice in tea once one gets used to it. I like it now, but did not at first.

What annoys one so is that one can go to any number of cafes, milk bars, etc., and consume as much milk as one like; yet in one's own home, where one wants it most, one is only allowed a half-pint, and now that is going to be cut. I like to make my own custards, junkets, milk puddings, etc., but household is not quite the same as fresh.

Why cannot the name of the dairy supplying five pints per head be disclosed? 'Utterly Disgusted' has only to report. One can only hope the Food Inspector saw the letter and will take action!

ANOTHER DISGUSTED

Cheltenham, 3rd September, 1946

Milk Manna

SIR – Hearing many stories about the wastage of milk at schools, I would like to suggest that those responsible for the handling of the milk in schools should be empowered, officially of course, to divide any pint of milk into two or more portions for any children who can only drink part of a pint. This would allow for the saving of many pints, which could be diverted to folk who receive no priority rations and have no family living with them. It would also mean an increased revenue, if that means anything nowadays.

MILK RATION

Dundee, 24th September 1947

Milky Misapprehension

SIR – Your correspondent 'Milk Ration,' like many others, is labouring under a misapprehension with regard to school milk. The quantity a child receives is one-third of a pink (a teacupful).

I might add that our milk ration—for two adults and one child over five—is one pint per day; once a week we get two pints. The odd thing is that my mother and sister, who are registered with a different milkman, get two pints per day. So people with children are not necessarily 'swimming' in milk.

PARENT

Dundee, 25th September, 1947

Milk for the Elderly

SIR – It seems to be the aim of this Government to kill off us elderly people by starvation. Rations have long been inadequate. Now we have not enough milk to make a small pudding. Surplus milk goes to make dried milk for babies who do not need it, and schoolchildren are stuffed with milk until they hate the sight of it. Cannot the elderly have light and appetising food which they can digest—milk, fresh eggs, butter, and an occasional chicken?

HUNGRY INVALID

Leeds, 17th February, 1949

Rancid Butter

SIR – The Oils and Fats Division of the Ministry of Food have informed me that a quantity of butter of manufacturing quality will be available for distribution to bakers and confectioners during the next rationing period. It will cost 265s a cwt.

It is emphasised that manufacturers will not have the option of selecting the type of butter they receive, and rejected deliveries will be replaced only if the Ministry is satisfied the butter was not fit for use at the time of delivery.

What is butter of manufacturing quality? Reputable manufacturers use only best-quality butter similar to that used by the housewife in the home.

Why should I pay the 265s a cwt. For it? That works out at 2s 4¼d a lb., and the subsidized price of butter in the shops is 1s 6d a lb.

My interpretation of the Ministry's circular is that they are overloaded with butter which is beginning to go bad, and they want to unload it on the manufacturers.

Many commodities have gone bad through being withheld from the consumers. Potatoes were an excellent example. Is butter another?

ALEX HENDERSON
Dundee, 30th July, 1949

Cut Butter Spread Margarine

SIR – I have been following the correspondence about the cut in the butter rations. I think the answer is to improve our margarine.

In Holland butter costs more than four shillings per pound and is used only as a treat on special occasions by most families. Dutch margarine tastes as good as our butter and everyone uses it as a matter of course.

Make margarine as good as it can be made to taste and it will sell readily and we will hear less grumbling about dear butter.

CA' CANNY WI' THE BUTTER!
Dundee, 5th September, 1950

8

Eggspectations

Eggs were in short supply in the war. In 1940 millions of hens had to be killed or sold for domestic keeping as there was a shortage of feed for commercial chicken farms. The resultant hen deficit led to a meagre ration of 1 egg per person per week, with expectant mothers and vegetarians allowed 2 eggs per week.

One could opt to raise chickens domestically and receive chicken feed rations in exchange for one's right to egg rations. Put out by the lack of commercial feed poultry specialists riled at this cottage chicken industry while the public was plied with American dried eggs.

Eggonomics

SIR – As a poultry farmer I am repeatedly asked why eggs are so scarce. May I be allowed to explain some of the causes? Before the war the number of eggs, either in shell or in liquid form, imported by this country was enormous, but for obvious reasons has now dwindled to a mere trickle. In pre-war days, poultry farmers all over the British Isles contributed in no small way to the supply of eggs. They were encouraged to do so by a public who were quick to appreciate the value of an absolutely fresh egg.

Since the war began poultry farmers have been frequently reminded that they were not to expect either help or encouragement from the Government and, in fact, were exhorted to curtail their stocks of poultry. Meantime foodstuffs were becoming scarce and their value rising so rapidly that eggs could not be sold at a price to cover cost of production.

It was not surprising, therefore, that poultry farmers began to kill off their birds. At first this reduction was imperceptible. For my own part, I began by culling every bird which I regarded as a doubtful producer. Frankly there should be very few 'doubtful' birds in a well-managed flock.

As time passed, and food became increasingly difficult to procure, I found myself sending to the poulterer many hens which in a normal time would be regarded as profitable layers. Incidentally, those birds met a very poor sale due to the fact that most poultry farmers in the locality were disposing of their birds at about the same time. Now that foodstuffs are so strictly and meagrely rationed I have been compelled to rid myself of still more layers, probably some of the best I have bred.

My stock is now a shadow of what it was. The majority of my poultry-houses are either empty or only partially filled. Most of my incubators are idle and my staff is depleted. My case is similar to that of hundreds of poultry farmers all over the country.

Lord Woolton has decreed that eggs are now to be sold at a price which is most certainly an uneconomic one from the producer's standpoint. This low price, if persisted in for any length of time, will compel an even further curtailment of stock, if not their total extinction.

It can be seen, therefore, how quickly and easily poultry stocks can be diminished, and as there can be no eggs without hens, or conversely, no hens without eggs, housewives need not look for any increase in either eggs or poultry for some time to come.

OVUM

Dundee, 26th February, 1941

Paltry Rations

SIR – Among the mysteries of the war which our former Minister of Agriculture, Mr W. S. Morrison, may care to explain, is why we poultry keepers should be rationed. Apart from corn, half the daily ration for poultry consists of middlings and bran. These come from the millers on whom poultry keepers, in fact, depend to keep going at all.

Bread is not rationed, so there must be enough flour and to spare. But if there is enough flour what has happened to the middlings and the bran which are what is left when the white flour is separated from the wheat?

It may be that they are replacing maize which used to be imported, or that they are being given to dairy cows. In either case, Mr. Morrison surely ought to have had the foresight to prepare adequate grain storage.

ERIC GRAY

Lewes, 7th March, 1941

Egg Raider

SIR – The rationing of eggs is not before time. To my certain knowledge a Sunderland tradesman who is in no way connected with the provision trade has been using his car at week-ends to collect scores of eggs from farms in the country, and has been disposing of them at 3s 6d per dozen in Sunderland. That trader does not subscribe to Christian doctrines.

ANONYMOUS

Sunderland, 4th June, 1941

Beaten Eggs

SIR – I have dealt in all rationed foods except meat since rationing started and have overcome many obstacles and complications, but this time I am beaten—on eggs.

I obtained 47 registrations. This being three short of the required 50, I have the unenviable task of inconveniencing my would-be customer by returning their counterfoils to register elsewhere to obtain their egg ration.

H. R. A.

Plymouth, 27th June, 1941

Shell Eggs

SIR – In times of peace members of the baking and confectionery trade were told they were assisting the home producer by the use of shell eggs. Under the egg-rationing scheme no provision has been made for the sale of shell eggs to the trade.

Bakers and confectioners who use nothing but shell eggs are apparently to be left without a supply of any egg product and up to the present they are not entitled to any share of available frozen eggs and products which are distributed to traders who are not in the habit of using shell eggs.

USER OF SHELL EGGS

Plymouth, 27th June, 1941

Border Knitters

I read in a certain weekly the other day that a 'man' was fined £3 for ill-treating his wife because she failed to provide an egg for his break-fast. Some folk say, 'He should have been given £3 instead of a fine', but I don't agree. I am afraid, now that eggs are to be rationed, if something is not done to increase our egg supply, there will be a few of our men-folk who will have to pay the £3 fine. Eggs are now being graded, polished and presented for sale, similar to apples, when apples were for sale.

Milk is also graded, i.e., T.T. and so on. If things continue in a similar direction much longer, one will require to go through a University training to enable one to buy the smallest commodity accurately!

ANONYMOUS

Selkirk, 17th July, 1941

Egg on Face

SIR – Your last two issues have contained criticisms of the recent Poultry Order which I, as chairman of the Chesterfield Branch of the Poultry Association of Great Britain (SPBA), and secretary and director of Chesterfield Poultry Producers (egg packing station), cannot leave unchallenged. No one would attempt to condone a policy which first encouraged the rearing of stock and later compelled its destruction, but it was the encouragement which deserved criticism.

I wonder what the newspaper world would have though had newsprint been reduced to one-eighth of pre-war requirements and at the same time hundreds of thousands of private people encouraged to publish their own news sheets? Early in 1940 millions of birds were taken out of the hands of specialists and put into the hands of backward novices—a wicked waste of the restricted supplies of feeding stuffs and definitely against the national interest.

'Domestics' were allowed food, which rightfully belonged to the community, to keep 12 hens and produce 1800 eggs per year against an official ration of 40. The new Order, which still allows 150 eggs appears to be exposing so-called patriotism as nothing more than sheer selfishness.

Under the original Order thousands of specialists were ruined, including many 1918 ex-Servicemen, and, to give a personal angle, my own stock has been reduced from 3000 to 800, with a further reduction in October—an infinitely more serious position than the one 'domestics' are now facing. From the viewpoint of a specialist producer and distributor, the Order is not as stupid as it might appear. It will achieve the desired object of a fairer distribution of eggs to the public and at the same time eliminate much of the present widespread use of valuable human food to produce backyard eggs.

WALTER FOULK

Chesterfield, 17th July 1942

Poultry Pinched

SIR – I listened to the Minister of Food broadcasting his sorrowful tale of the need for further ration cuts owing to the world food shortage. Apparently the flour extraction rate is to go up to 85 percent again, which means darker bread and less feeding-stuffs for pigs and poultry.

Farmers who had planned on the strength of a promise of increased feeding stuffs to supply us with extra fresh pork, bacon and eggs have now to cancel their plans, and prospects of a more interesting diet fade away into the dim and distant future, together with many other Government promises.

Our Socialist Minister on his recent trip to the United States does not seem to have been very successful in persuading our American friends to adopt any form of personal food rationing in order to release more food for this country or the Continent.

After his catalogue of woe he was so rash as to admit that it was the desire to conserve our foreign currency which was behind the decision to deprive the harassed housewife of the dried eggs. For the sake of saving £25,000,000 per annum—less than 1s. per month per head of our population—our diet is to become even more austere, and our children, who need the valuable body-building properties of the eggs must go without.

M. L. JAMES

Plymouth, 8th February, 1946

Woman Food Minister

SIR – Many people will agree that the Ministry of Food would be better if a woman Minister was at the head. I do not believe that any woman could have so miscalculated as to consider any payment too large for supplies of the very valuable basic food, dried egg, in these days of rationing. Nor would a woman Minister have supported the scheme of the population inquiry at the present time at the excessive cost recently published. Words fail me to express my feelings

about the ridiculous promise of twice the amount of shell
eggs per month, especially when I recall how often the egg has
been bad.

MRS ANNE BELL

Leeds, 25th February, 1946

Fewer Eggs and Poultry

SIR – So the slaughter has begun! We all knew the darker loaf
meant less milk and beef, fewer eggs. Last Monday the
commercial poultry-keepers' rations were halved.

Where are the winter eggs and Xmas poultry to come
from? Are hundreds of tons of poultry food going to France
every week? The latest returns for May last show we sent the
staggering sum of £92,560 worth of animal feeding-stuffs
abroad against £3,746 in May of last year. Why do we do this?

We pay an enormous sum of money for dried egg coming
thousands of miles, for which the housewife has to give up
eight precious points per packet. Is this a policy of robbing
Peter to pay Paul?

I am sure your readers would be glad to see more shell
eggs, easy to digest, quick to prepare and above all, light on
precious fuel.

MRS M. SKELDING

Plymouth, 9th July, 1946

Sale of Starlings

SIR – Please allow me to join in the protest against the many
displays of starlings on poulterers' slabs. The mating season
has already begun for these birds, and the tiny scrap of meat
from each dead starling is of small value compared with the
work of a live bird in ridding us of insects and grubs. If the
public will refuse to buy these small birds, trappers and
poulterers, will be discouraged from this shameful trade.

W. G. S.

Leeds, 25th March, 1947

Woeful Record

SIR – Surely this Government should go down to posterity as the 'Woe! Woe!' Government, as scarcely a day passes without some rise in prices or some cut being announced:

Dried eggs 1/9 to 2/6 and 10 points; coffee 2d. a lb. dearer; biscuits to cost more; tea ration may be reduced; meat supplies to be 'dramatically' reduced in the autumn; imports of food to be reduced soon; price of cigarettes goes up 1/- a packet.

WOEFUL WON

Cheltenham, 18th April, 1947

CCCP Chicks

SIR – Today I received the following letter: 'Because of the need of urgency, the feeding stuffs coupons for pigs and poultry recently sent to you were issued without reference to current stock numbers. The pig and poultry stock on your holding at December 4, 1947, does not justify the issue made, and coupons to the value of ½ unit protein and 1¾ units cereal for each of the months January to April 1948, should, therefore, be returned to the department at your earliest convenience. Department of Agriculture for Scotland, Animal Feeding Stuffs branch, &c. D.E. 14395/1/71 500 1/48R.'

My fowls have eaten the January rations. I thought they had a USSR look about them. Must be that surplus Russian grain. From now on all cackling and crowing stops.

JOHN LAING

Dundee, 2nd February, 1948

Inefficient Eggs

SIR – When the Minister of Food stated the other day that the shortage of eggs was due to the habits of the hen, a Tory M.P suggested that these habits could be controlled by man. The Minister was not impressed.

It is not generally realised by the egg-eating public that the Tory MP was dead right. A capable poultryman, with the necessary equipment, can get more eggs from his flock in the autumn and winter months than he can in spring.

From October 1 up to and including to-day's collection, my own flock of 95 in February hatched pullets and 60 season hen, have laid an average of 91 eggs a day. Few flocks do better than this even in spring.

I am not boasting for such production is about normal for a flock handled by a specialist egg farmer, and there are hundreds of them in the country and empty poultry houses lying idle and rotting.

The cause of this is the idiotic rationing of feeding stuffs. If rationing cannot be abolished altogether, a system on the 'Food for eggs' principle should be adopted. Let there be a four-fold increase in the bonus allowance even at the expense of a reduction in the basic ration. The result would be millions more eggs for the public and the disappearance of the 'Black Market'. I am constantly being offered anything up to 10s. for a dozen eggs, and I admit that it is not altogether my conscience that keeps me from falling by the wayside, but the fact that to feed the number of birds I now have I must get the maximum bonus allowance of food, meagre though it be.

On the present system of rationing, a man whose flock of 100 birds produces only 30 eggs a day gets the same basic allowance as a man with the same number of birds producing up to 70 eggs a day. To return to the 'Black Market' the high cost of food stuffs makes the high price offered for eggs very tempting to the less capable poultryman whose flock is not doing so well, and in his case I doubt very much if honesty is the best policy.

A. REITH

Portsmouth, 14th December, 1950

Poor Eggsecution

SIR – There seems to be something far wrong with the egg

rationing system. Here in Dundee it's a big week when we're given two for each person, while in Pitlochry—only fifty miles away—anyone can have as many dozens as they want. They are priced 4s 6d per dozen in several shop windows.

DISGUSTED

Dundee, 22nd May, 1951

Dried Eggs

SIR – It was brought to our notice by some of our members that dried egg was displayed for sale in open containers at 10s per lb.

We took this up with the Ministry of Food (MOF), who replied as follows: 'It is contrary to Egg Products (Control and Maximum Prices) Order, 1946, to sell dried egg loose by retail for household consumption.'

We understand that bakers have been warned by the MOF to curtail to a minimum the use of dried egg in cake, as the present supplies have been so long in storage.

ELIZABETH M. PATTULLO

Dundee, 12th November, 1951

Eggs Fresh and Otherwise

SIR – Reading in the *Courier* this morning that we had six thousand-odd snoopers, I'm wondering if the Ministry of Food couldn't send some of them to find out why the egg in the ration are more often rotten than fresh.

I had six eggs for which I paid 2s 6d. Three were really bad, the other three were queries. I put them all in the dustbin.

The MOF, which is supposed to be a highly hygienic organisation, should not be allowed to sell these eggs. I've come to the conclusion that half the illness in the country springs from these eggs.

I don't blame anyone going after fresh eggs if they are to

be found. At least something could be done to let us have
them fresh at 5s a dozen.

ANONYMOUS

Dundee, 23rd June 1952

Eggspensive

SIR – It is extraordinary the different angles from which this
subject is viewed. First, the man who claims that the whole
business of handling, etc., only costs 3d a dozen; followed up
by the poultrykeeper pointing out that, with the prices he has
to pay for feed, he is not getting nearly enough for his outlay.

Then I have come across the person who has no call to
come under the pool and states that it costs 4d to place that
stamp on an egg. Finally comes the dried egg idea—again a
help no doubt in a lean time but a poorer substitute for the
real thing.

What about going back to good old-time free trade—every
hen owner his own merchant, selling to the highest bidder.
Poultrykeepers and farmers have their cars, and transport
should present no difficulty.

Alternatively, the Housewives' Association and others
could set about doing what the New York wives did once
when eggs there reached a fantastic price—resolved to stop
buying for two weeks. Eggs went back to former figures at the
end of a week.

R. A. MURRAY

Dundee, 14th August, 1953

9

Onions and Oranges

Fruit was a rare commodity during the war. Oranges and clementines were prized luxuries though few could get their hands on them as priority went to children and pregnant women. Lemons and bananas all but disappeared and the peacetime return of the banana to Britain was met with great fanfare. Many members of the public struggled with the concept of vitamins and minerals that these exotic fruits were meant to provide. Many instead sought the fruit as juicy treats to spruce up the monotony of wartime cuisine, something the pricey onion did well too.

Onion Profiteering

SIR – I read with special interest your remarks referring to the present onion prices.

If, at any time you are in doubt as to the profit we, as retailers, get, I shall only be too pleased to furnish you with the prices we pay for any article, and also back it up with invoices.

This will enable you to arrive at the profit we obtain, and will, perhaps, dispel from your own mind the 'bogey' of profiteering, that a majority of the public would like to pin upon us.

Ask anything you like relative to our trade, and it will be truthfully answered and proved to you.

W. OXSPRING

Derby, 8th October, 1940

Rare Onions

SIR – I think it is about time something was done about the unequal distribution of goods.

As you are well aware, onions have been very short for months. I have been in the fruit trade for over 20 years, yet I cannot buy a single onion out of the cargo that was landed just lately, yet another firm in the town can get enough onions to supply the needs of everyone and have some left over. This is from your own report.

I was in London on Wednesday last and tried to obtain some of this rare commodity. I was told by a salesman in Covent Garden that if I was regular customer and would like to buy 10 nets of cauliflower at 3s. more than the market value I could have one box of onions. This I refused to do.

The Government expect everyone to keep on paying rates, and so on, as usual but how can the small shopkeeper do this?

I can tell the public what happens to tinned goods when they are controlled. The firms who have stocks just take them off sale and sell them to hotels, cafes, and so on, at the full price that the shopkeeper is allowed to sell at, thereby making extra profit and depriving the public of the goods.

It is time that a better system was adopted so that all the shops have a share of everything.

W. JOHNSON

Derby, 8th October, 1940

Garden Depredations

SIR – I fully agree with your correspondent, Mr. W. Mackay, that we should all of our utmost to grow food, but those who rifle the produce when grown should be punished. Last year, along with many others in the Nottingham-road district, we had our whole garden cleared.

Boys came along armed with bags and baskets, stripped all fruit trees, &c., and took everything eatable, many of the apples being thrown in the road after one bite had been taken. I am told that, as things are, these youths, if caught and prosecuted, are just given a caution. I hope and trust our local MPs will urge that sterner measures be meted out to these garden thieves. Otherwise many will fail to 'dig for victory'.

PATRIOT

Nottingham, 7th April, 1941

Black Oranges

SIR – Regarding the defeating of the 'Black Market' I would like to give my experience as to oranges. I went into a greengrocer's one afternoon last week, where a lady with a car stood waiting. The greengrocer returned from the back premises with a large bag, holding at least a dozen oranges, which he gave her with other purchases. She added 'I will send in my order towards the weekend'. I then asked if he had any for me. He said they had all gone. Coming out, I told someone living opposite this shop, who said they had seen three crates taken in the same afternoon.

Why would they be allowed to save them just for a few favoured customers, instead of all getting a chance?

FAIRPLAY

Nottingham, 26th June, 1941

Don't Go off Your Onions

SIR – Many fruiterers are in a difficulty in the matter of onions, having received their supply. The public in many cases are not collecting their rations. There is a danger of the onions not keeping too long, and it is a vital necessity that food should not be wasted. The only alternative is for the fruiterer to sell to any customers if this waste is to be avoided. We have gone to a lot of trouble to work this scheme so that the public should all get a fair share. Also we cannot afford the loss it will entail if they are allowed to go to waste. It is up to the public to collect their rations, and thus help the fruiterers and save a valuable food being wasted. Don't go off your onion.

A. JACKSON, RETAIL FRUIT TRADE FEDERATION

Nottingham, 29th October, 1941

Brierfield Raiders

SIR – Last week thousands of oranges were displayed at my greengrocers, but what happened? My children have not seen an orange for twelve months. It is always the same tale. Too late. But why let greedy people from Brierfield, Nelson and Colne get them? They are not satisfied to get them from their own stores but must come and get ours. Our growing children should get their share.

The manager told me that the older children would get theirs after five days. The whole stock was cleared out in half a day! I am sick of being refused. I would appeal to mothers in Brierfield, Nelson, Colne and Padiham to keep off our orange supply so that our own children can get ours. No doubt your shops get their quota, and I, for one, would not dream of coming to your shops to try to deprive you of your share.

M. F. ROBERTS

Burnley, 28th February, 1942

Backroom Oranges

SIR – Fresh fruit, in particular oranges, is an important health-giving item of the human diet, especially that of children. Rationing does not seem to have effected a fair and unprejudiced distribution of this wartime delicacy. Too often I see oranges in the houses, where I know no children live!

One further item. Recent access to the 'back-room' of a grocery stores disclosed two large clothes-baskets replete with oranges the skins of which were already dry and shrivelled. When my wife inquired for the rations of two of our children of 'orange-ration age' she was informed that 'we have no supplies!' Yet there seems to be no scarcity among the adult population! Why?

UNIVERSITY GRADUATE

Plymouth, 27th March, 1942

Sunday Refreshments

SIR – Your correspondent, Mr R. A. Yellowless, hero of several 'lost causes' has misinterpreted the main purport of my letter on the above subject. He strikes off at a very decided tangent in a very fussy diatribe on the most lamentable scarcity of those delectable commodities, ice-cream, lemonade and oranges. He also adjures me to 'get the war finished, show my patriotism by keeping up my spirits' 'thank heaven for numberless blessings' etc., etc. Then he commits the unpardonable sin of 'worrying' my non-de-plume (French, Mr Yellowless).

Mr Yellowless, I believe, is, as usual, in the minority, but lest that be not so, allow me to state my grouse is on account of the alarming growth of bureaucratic control, the outcome of which is, that initiative in business and commerce is strangled, and instead of being cogs in the great wheels of those vital and integral spheres, ordinary business men have become as clay in the hands of the potter, victims of restrictions, and suffering from an acute sense of frustration at every turn. I was gratified to read in the Press recently that even Sir Archibald Sinclair agrees that the bureaucrats must be debunked 'après la guerre' (French Mr Yellowless).

RESURGAM

Selkirk, 24th September, 1942

Fruiterers and the Oranges

SIR – After a lot of experience of the difficulties and details we have to adhere to, I say frankly that the method of distribution of oranges could be improved upon a great deal. I myself actually had customers from Sutton-in-Ashfield,

Bulwell, even Weston-super-Mare. Yet we are expected to supply them if they have green ration books.

Meanwhile, owing to the small supplies our regular customers have to be told 'Sorry sold out'. All fruiterers and greengrocers know the people who 'trot round from shop to shop' in order to get supplies, not only of oranges, but any scarce commodity. We know this fraternity too well, as being the cause of a great deal of trouble and unnecessary labour. Some satisfactory scheme could surely be evolved whereby shopkeepers would be in a position to supply their regular customers and also customers who keep to their regular shops for scarce commodities.

E.T. ADAMS

Nottingham, 1st June, 1943

Orange Peel Mystery

SIR – My recent note on possible uses for orange peel uses reminds a correspondent of what he calls the classics mystery in the long history of this fruit. 'Have you yet discovered what Doctor Samuel Johnson did with his orange peel?' he asks.

It was one of the learned Doctor's 'particularities' that he kept in his pocket the Seville oranges from which he had squeezed the juice for his drink. Boswell persistent if not impertinent won a small bet from Lady Diana Beauclerk by daring to ask the great man what he did with the peel. He found that Johnson scraped it 'very neatly', cut it into pieces and dried it, but beyond that he could discover nothing. Even Boswell's assumption of 'a mock solemnity' and his declaration that 'the world must be left in the dark' if the Doctor could not be prevailed upon to tell drew from Johnson only the blank finality of this statement; 'Nay, Sit you could say it more emphatically: he could not be prevailed upon even by his dearest friends to tell'.

The mystery now assumes a larger proportion. If we only knew what Johnson did with his dried orange peel, what benefit might not be drawn into the resources of our war effort?

NORTHERNER II

Leeds, 2nd February, 1944

Overrated Oranges

SIR – For not so many years oranges have come to this country and for only a short period have grapefruits been known here.

In both instances the juice only is of value (apart from a limited quantity of marmalade). The juice is a very small percentage of the whole. The bulk is a mass of waste. Why is the enormous amount of sea and land tonnage with all the labour, fuel, etc., used for transport? The country is supposed to be very short of such facilities for vital necessities, also repatriation of troops, internees and war-weary people.

All the juice could be carried in suitable containers with a fraction of transport, labour and fuel now being used, Exports could then be increased. Practical knowledge and experience in this case, as in so many other industries seem to be quite secondary to the desire to shine in verbosity

SUCKER

Cheltenham, 31st December, 1945

The Orange Dump

SIR – I strongly support Mr J. G. Law's statement re the orange dump at Hessle. I myself have witnessed thousands of oranges in perfect condition being reclaimed. Apart from that, surely the timber was worth something.

Shopkeepers are making a charge of 6d and 8d for the empty boxes, and as I have been given to understand that there are 22,000 of them dumped here surely these could be turned to good used for the Red Cross.

R. WOODALL

Hull, 18th March, 1944

No Bananas

SIR – Isn't it rather unfair that only those holding children's ration books should get bananas? Many adults have longed for them, as they have been used to having them, whereas children do not even know what they are, therefore cannot miss them.

They are such a help, as one can make a nice tasty dish with them, but, again, the mothers of children will benefit if their children don't like them. The home without a family must do without, and the old people, who thought they were going to have something different for a change.

Why not let the children have the oranges while the older people could have the bananas? After all, surely they are entitled to something tasty.

FAIRPLAY

Dundee, 10th November, 1945

Banana Booby Trap

SIR – The arrival in Yorkshire of the first post-war supplies of bananas has produced its inevitable crop of anecdotes, dealing, for the most part, with the reactions of the very young to this unaccustomed delicacy. One story comes from Bradford, where, it is said, an excited small boy, his mouth full of memories of the ice-cream he had last summer, rushed into a green-grocer's shop and, holding out an empty banana skin, asked for it to be refilled.

But I like better the tale told me by one of my colleagues upon whose youthful son the chemical properties of the banana appear to have had a most sinister effect. Having eaten the fruit, he gazed contemplatively for a moment or two at the empty skin, and then rose, full of purpose, from the table.

'Oh, dear' he said 'Banana skins. People slip on these'. And he made his way out into the street, with mischief in his eye.

NORTHERNER II

Leeds, 25th February, 1946

Unseen Bananas

SIR – I notice in the *Echo* that Cheltenham is to receive a second allocation of bananas.

Would it be too much to ask that this allocation should, in the first instance, be made to those kiddies who have not yet seen one?

My boy, aged three, is still waiting, like many others. I suggest that a very simple method would be a notice in your widely-read columns, stating the exact date of issue to the shops, and that the sale on the first day be restricted to the holders of green ration-books not yet marked.

Even if it takes a few days to deliver the bananas, I see no reason why the shops could not sell from a date specified, as surely the bananas would keep a few days?

Perhaps someone is having to do with the distribution of fruit from overseas will notice my letter and give the unlucky kiddies a chance this time.

D. M. BROOKES

Cheltenham, 20th March, 1946

Banana Republic

SIR – How perfectly bizarre! Expectant mothers can now get bananas provide the sales are recorded on R.B.7 ration book by marking the number of the allocation on the Z coupons on page 13—or is it 14? I forget.

Why cannot we all buy them like they do in every other country—in big bunches off barrows whenever we want them? I suppose officials and forms are so much more 'posh'—and totalitarian.

F. GORDON HARPER

Plymouth, 2nd September 1947

Bananas or Meat?

SIR – Being without any political prejudices and having

recently returned home from a visit to the United States by one of the few remaining 'banana boats'.

The ship I travelled in, a 5,000 tonner, brought home 3,000 tons of meat, plus 11 passengers. I understand that the majority of vessels of this type are engaged carrying this essential article of good, although perhaps some people may prefer bananas! Many people think these to be a greatly over-rated foodstuff, difficult to handle and more difficult to keep from quickly deteriorating.

In any case, any advantage derived by their use by expectant mothers would appear to be extremely doubtful; one would think that a general all-round increase in their rations would be beneficial.

F.C. BARRETT

Plymouth, 5th September, 1947

10

Meagre Meat

Meat was one of the few rationed foodstuffs to be rationed by price, and not weight, in an attempt to curb a flourishing black-market trade and an acknowledgement of the different quality in cuts. The meat supply dwindled as acres of pastureland were repurposed for arable crops. As farmers were encouraged to produce wheat and not meat thousands of householders formed pig clubs.

A group of houses would jointly feed pigs out of household scraps and then share in the meat after mandatorily selling half of the pig's carcass to the government. Pig clubs were a way to escape feeble butcher sausages whose trace-like meat content prompted the government to require that sausages contain at least 10% meat. Meat pies were filled almost entirely filled with American Spam. Facing a dearth of succulent meat the British public were enraged by the government's decision to not procure foreign meat at the war's end.

Meat Heads

SIR – Many like myself may have spent an hour or two in the Food Controller's office to-day, feeling all the while that, unless we are bombed out, the food control, like the coal control, would fizzle out from incompetence.

Obviously the two meat coupons (divided into two) will

have to be withdrawn and substituted by meal coupons, three a day. The ration book, on page 3, par. 9, tells us 'half' a meat or bacon coupon may be used to obtain a cooked meal of rationed meat or bacon in any hotel, restaurant, café, tea shop, etc., and the half coupon must be detached from the ration book by the person serving the meal.'

Seven, or even five or six, days into four coupons won't go and leave anything over for Sunday.

ARITHMETIC

Leeds, 12 January 1940

Meaty Moses

SIR – Just 41 years ago this week I remember drawing my rations, a couple of biscuits and a small amount of horseflesh, and how little it seemed on which to exist for the ensuing 24 hours.

I have just seen (discovered would be more appropriate) my 1s. 2d. meat ration allowance on which I must exist for seven days, and I am forced to the conclusion that we were overfed in Ladysmith.

SIEGE WALLAH

Leeds, 28th February, 1941

The Cottager and His Pig

SIR – Among the many improvement to be placed to the credit of the present Government is the encouragement to keep a pig for family consumption. Scattered all over England to-day are disused pigsties. Subsidy for building, rebuilding and repairing of pigsties would be helpful. Many a poor countryman and townsman may look longingly at ruined pigsties.

The pig club, with its insurance against loss, and its facilities for obtaining pig rations, its speakers and its organisers, is of great practical service to the community. The thrifty householder, with an eye to a better fed family and nation, realises the advantage of the pig as a provider of fresh and salt meat (bacon, ham, pork, chaps, brawn or souse, chine, spare-rib, sausage, fry, etc.).

Trusting that this may interest the many readers of your popular and widely-circulated paper.

GEORGINA SNOWDEN

Chesterfield, 7th March, 1941

Millers' Rash

SIR – Now that livestock feeders are faced with even further cuts in their rations, it is worth considering whether the quality of the compound foods is as good as it might be. Before the war, pig-feeders could achieve bacon weight in six months or less. This now takes seven or even eight months. Dairy meals fed at the old rate produce less than they did, and other rations are not so efficient. It may be a coincidence, but this deterioration in the quality of balanced rations dates from just about the time when the Government laid down standard formulas for these, which millers are bound to observe when making up meals, cakes, etc. Is it not possible that the millers understand their job better than anyone else?

GEORGE HILLYAR

Selkirk, 24th April, 1941

Livestock

SIR – The new livestock rationing period started on May 1, but many farmers are only now receiving their coupons. Why the delay? Why withhold the bricks until we have started to build the house? The season is late this year, and most of this quarter's rations will be wanted for the first few weeks of it. Yet Gloucestershire millers' warehouses are crammed with feeding-stuffs which they are only too anxious to supply but cannot do so without coupons.

C. KEABLE

Cheltenham, 17th May, 1941

Power of Bacon

SIR – Farm workers should supplement their food rations by keeping pigs. With another arduous season before them these men will need to be fighting fit, and pig-keeping is one of the ways in which they can secure energy-producing foods.

Some farmers, remembering what an older generation of workers could do on a breakfast of fat bacon, have already provided their men with sties; in some cases even a little ground to grow potatoes, Belgian carrots, artichokes, and other suitable food for their pigs. Mr. Hudson's hope that other employers will follow suit is not, I am sure likely to be disappointed.

CEDRIC DREWE

Exeter and Plymouth Gazette, 27th February, 1942

Should Rabbits Be Rationed?

SIR – May I suggest to the Food Controller that rabbits be rationed. On several occasions I have stood in queues for a rabbit, only to find that there were not enough to go round. There is nothing more dis-heartening than to stand hours in a queue and then not get anything. Why not distribute the rabbits to the butchers' shops. We can trust our butcher to see that they are fairly shared out among the customers, even if we only get one a month. As it is people come in from colliery districts grab their own share and other people's as well.

LIVE AND LET LIVE

Sunderland, 22nd January, 1943

British Restaurants

SIR – It was announced the other day that townspeople who assisted with harvesting this year are to have double meat ration. It seems a strange state of affairs that farmers and farm labourers have worked long hours each day through the winter producing precious food and rearing and feeding animals with only an extra cheese ration, and the townspeople who are to come and help in summer require and are to have a double meat ration. The latter are used to having so many more privileges, such as cafes and British restaurants that are not available to their country cousins. Farm workers have been among the poorest paid of manual labourers.

FARM WORKER

Nottingham, 2nd April, 1943

North South Divide

SIR – May I reply to the letters in which your correspondents allege that people in the south of England get an unfairly large share of Scotch beef, whisky, etc. As a Scotswoman who lives in the south of England, may I say that this is simply not true. Our meat varies in quality, but is usually second-rate. If what I put on my table most Sundays is Scotch beef, it's no credit to Scotland. We get no pies, bridies with which to augment our rations, and we never see the rissoles and prepared meats that appear plentifully in many Scottish shops. Where I live macaroni, biscuits, salad cream, dried fruit, cakes are usually unobtainable, and our selection of sweets and tinned goods compares very unfavourably with the displays in the Dundee shops. Your correspondents grudge the southerners, but say nothing of the southerners' heroic acceptance of their very large share of bombs, flying bombs, and robots. I am, by the way, as fond of Scotland as anyone who ever postured in front of a flag emblazoned with the rampant lion.

HELAN HAMES

Dundee, 20th July, 1945

Child Portions

SIR – Regarding the cut in the fat ration not to effect school canteens for children, I would like to be advised, if possible, as to what becomes of the children with no canteen. With all respect to the canteen and their helpers, I think every child should have the equivalent to each other, and they need it.

G. M. LATHAM

Hull, 26th February, 1946

Mealy Puddings

SIR – Dr Edith Summerskill, parliamentary secretary at the Ministry of Food, said that haggis would remain unrationed. Mealy puddings came within the definition of flour confectionery and would require the surrender of B.U. coupons. The decision that haggis would remain unrationed was not taken to prevent an uprising in Scotland, but because haggis contained the heart, lungs and liver of sheep chopped up with suet, onions, and oatmeal, while mealy pudding contained oatmeal and fat, which was the reasons why it was flour confectionery. Col. Gomme-Duncan (Con., Perth and Kinross) congratulated the honourable lay on having given the first real definition of haggis.

ANONYMOUS

Dundee, 24th July, 1946

Thieves among the Pigeons

SIR – A new crime which is increasing at Pallion is pigeon and poultry stealing. Early this morning I found that seven out of eight pigeons had been stolen out of the backyard. They are fantails, and pets of my three children.

VICTIM

Sunderland, 28th October, 1946

Famous Sausage

SIR – I was interested in Mrs Rae's letter on the meat ration in England. I quite agree with her. I lived with my family near London during the war, and never once in that long period did we see the famous sausage; on very rare occasions we were able to obtain some liver.

Furthermore, the bakers' shops had nothing to offer but bread. I was amazed to see cakes, teabread, &c., one year when home on holiday. Later my sister obliged by sending us food parcels.

May I add, the only thing plentiful and off the ration was bombs and sirens.

MIMA WELLS

Dundee, 21st October, 1948

Fawn and Flatter

SIR – I have tried to reason out why I, doubtless in common with countless others, invariably obtain rough skin and gristle for the bit of meat ration. What really does happen to the sirloin, undercut, pinbone, steak, kidneys, liver, sweetbreads, etc.? Similarly the queer bit of cheese and bacon ration usually rank in taste and smell; it seems more like flotsam which may have floated in with the food imports.

Is it possible that some of our shopkeepers fawn and flatter those with money. For instance, the extreme scarcity of cooking fats does not worry the likes of these people who can get plenty of cooking oil at about 15/- per bottle.

T. PROMISE

Wells, 21st May, 1948

The Meat We Eat

SIR – I wonder if anybody else shared my amazement the other night to hear Sir John Boyd Orr's statement that the meat consumption in these islands was only 10 per cent. down in 1939. What utter poppycock! The ration was introduced in 1939 at a level of 2s. 2d. when meat was of good quality. To-day, the fresh meat ration stands at 10d., with much of the meat inferior grade. And then he goes on to infer that the available meat is shared more equally these days, to the benefit of the lower-wage class. These are the days of statistics, but if figures can be made to prove a statement like this, then there is no limit to belief. Ask the local butcher; ask the housewife next door; better still, ask yourself.

G. EDDOWES

The Nottingham, 14th June, 1948

Cut 'Meals Out' Meat Before the Ration!

SIR – Housewives are being continually told all sorts of reasons why our meat ration is now cut down to less than 1½d. a day. There is something about it that doesn't ring true to the ordinary citizen. I still wish to know why a good meal of meat can be obtained in any restaurant throughout the whole of the country, providing an average of 3s. is paid.

Canteens can also supply a good meat meal daily to thousands of workers, and rightly so. Dinner at hotels is supplied nightly to any Association of 100 or more.

Yet, we housewives are asked to be content to feed our families on a miserable ration of 1½d. per day per person. Must we suffer indefinitely, or shall we be driven to the extreme measures of the suffragettes in order to get something accomplished?

EDITH F. CRUWYS

Cheltenham, 21st March, 1949

Could Kick Strachey

SIR – It is a fact that miners get 1s worth of meat extra, on top of the ordinary ration, making 1s 8d. Besides this the best joints of beef and pork, rabbits, suet, offal all go to the pit canteens, also special pies full of meat. I was wondering whether the miners would share some of this with my husband and three hungry sons who look to me for food. I am helpless to do anything about it except write this letter.

I could kick Strachey for refusing the Irish beef at 10d a lb. because he wanted it for 8d a lb. Then he lets Holland buy it and sell it back to us in tins for 3s 6d a lb. I call that good business – on Holland's part.

Even when we had a war to keep going we could get spam, pork, dried egg at half the price, dried milk for cooking, 'cigs' at half the price, pictures at half to-day's prices and 1s 4d worth of meat a week.

THAT'S ALL

Sunderland, 6th April, 1949

Bulk Buy

SIR – The Ministry are solely responsible for providing an adequate meat ration. Why should the butcher, who is not responsible, have to assume responsibility? We, the meat retailers, are not being unreasonable. All we want is to satisfy our customers and to work our business diligently and legitimately, and earn for our staff and ourselves a reasonable standard of living to which we are justly entitled.

EDWARD PIGGOT, MASTER BUTCHERS' ASSOCIATION

Dundee, 16th December, 1950

Flying Pigs

SIR – In the New Year the meat ration will be cut to below even what it was in the darkest days of the War, and most of us, I suppose, would prefer to suffer this than to be held to ransom by the Argentine or any other foreign Government. But would this appalling state of affairs ever have arisen if the withering hand of Whitehall had not been allowed to contaminate our joint, and if the meat trade had been left to do its own buying in the markets of the world? Is not this starvation level in meat the result of the inefficiency of our own Government who seems to know as little about the meat market as a pig knows about flying?

SCRAG-END

Wells, 22nd December, 1950

Butchered

SIR – The customer and retailer are sick tired of control. What is our best way out of this maze? We wonder if our Government are really serious in their opposition to Communism.

KEN MURRAY, MASTER FLESHER

Dundee, 6th January, 1951

Meat Headache

SIR – Another cut in the meat ration. The Government have nothing to offer us but austerity—less food, less coal, electricity cuts, higher taxation, and goodness knows what next. Socialism has brought nothing but worry and headaches to the British people.

ANOTHER HOUSEWIFE

Dundee, 30th January, 1951

Extinct Meat

SIR – The high price of meat is the Government's excuse for our nearly extinct meat ration, yet in the next breath they tell us that they are going to give the butchers a subsidy to make up for their decrease in business. This really amounts to putting the butcher on the dole, and at the same time admitting their own incompetence as buyers.

CITIZEN

Leeds, 1st February, 1951

Sausage Dogs

SIR – A sample of some sausage I bought to-day. Words fail me when I try to describe the taste. The dog was hungry, but when I offered her some, she just sniffed and walked away. The so-called sausages ended up in the dustbin and bang goes another 1s. 4d. Socialists are very fond of recalling the Tories' soup kitchens, but an unemployed man derived more nourishment from that soup, than we do to-day from some the expensive rubbish we have had to eat since this Government took office.

A. SMITH

Portsmouth, 23rd April, 1951

Meatiocrity

SIR – What is wrong with the Argentine's offer to deal directly with Smithfield?—can it be the Government are ashamed to admit that practical men would show up more of the Government officials' inefficiency? One thing I am sure of, Smithfield experts could fix reasonable buying prices sooner, and make sure they got value for their money.

Away with dictatorship. A great many of our countrymen died fighting dictatorship in the hope it would be abolished for ever, yet here we are in Britain, the only country still rationed and under-rationed at that, for meat. Let us be finished with being told what and how much we will eat, and when we will eat it.

HARASSED BUTCHER

Dundee, 5th April, 1951

Belgian Ham

SIR – When Mr Webb became Minister of Food he spoke loftily of giving us 'a little of what we fancy' now and again.

Being one who would gladly exchange my bacon ration for boiled ham once in a while, but not registered with a grocer who can provided it, I thought I was in luck last Friday when, in a Union Street Aberdeen shop, I noticed cooked ham being sliced.

Yes, non-registered customers were being served, so I asked for half a pound. Mercifully, for my pocket, the assistant mentioned the price—12/6 a pound! He said it was Belgian ham. I bought a pork pie instead.

SINGE RATION

Aberdeen, 17th November, 1950

Skinflint

SIR – There is legitimate ground for deep dissatisfaction by the butcher. Profits for the butcher are determined by a mysterious band of people at the ministry called 'the costings division.' They decide the degree of poverty the trade should endure.

Many butchers are concerned at the ever-increasing cost of sausage skins—a headache for the butcher even to contemplate making 'sausages!'

I wish the Government 'planners' could, or would, stand behind a butcher's counter for one week and bear the brunt of the consumer's discontent.

But cheer up, fold, you will have corned beef for your Christmas dinner. Your weekly ration as from December 10 until further notice, is as follows:—Is 2d worth of carcase meat and 4d worth of canned corned meat.

HARASSED BUTCHER

Dundee, 13th December, 1950

Meat Mess

SIR – I was astounded to read and hear over the wireless the statement of the government to us butchers, through our Federation, to do all in our power during this difficult period. Why only a few months back they threatened us in a way unheard of in a free country. We are at their mercy with the type of meat they dish out to us and they even accused us of unfair trading. Are we not having manufacturing meat to be sold as ration meat, thereby obtaining money by the false pretences from the customer, on behalf of the M.O.F., to get them out of a mess?

W. T. MILLBANK

Portsmouth, 22nd December, 1950

Argentine Steak

SIR – The price the Argentine are asking for their meat is not exorbitant in view of present world prices. Our trade journal quotes a national daily paper as stating, 'In 1948-49 the profit on imported meat to the M.O.F was £2,860,000 but the subsidy on home-killed meat, however, was £35,778,000'. In view of our present miserable ration is there any justification for the expenditure of this enormous sum? I am sure the average housewife would not mind. She might even avoid wasting her money on this ewe mutton we are seeing so much of.

B. OAWSON

Portsmouth, 5th January, 1951

Shmucks

SIR – Surely the Minister is not serious when he says that we cannot expect to pick and choose our joint. What does he take us housewives for, a lot of stupid people? We have not been able to do that for the past 10 years.

UNDERCUT

Portsmouth, 5th January, 1951

Making Bacon

SIR – After listening to a broadcast given by a farmer on how the bacon ration can't be increased may I give an opinion? Farmers put many obstacles in the way of feeding pigs for the country but they always manage to feed them for their own use, and in Berwickshire alone I doubt if there could be found one farmhouse where there isn't the remains of a pig hanging from the ceiling with one or two more in the sty ready to take its place. The Government should make it a condition that if farmers want to continue enjoying this luxury they will have to contribute to the nation's larder with so many pigs a year, thus giving us all a share. Otherwise, make them exist as we do with porridge or tea and toast alone for breakfast.

STREAKY

Berwick upon Tweed, 18th January, 1949

Bacon Sandwiches

SIR – While shopping in a Leeds store I went to the café for a cup of tea, and was amazed to hear a customer ask for a bacon sandwich; so along with about 50 others, I did likewise and was astounded at the amount of beautiful lean bacon that went into those sandwiches. Come on housewives of Leeds! How long are you going to watch food being diverted into luxury lunches?

MAYVILLE

Leeds, 25th March, 1947

11

Fish or Fowl

The meat ration strained traditional supplies of chicken, beef and lamb encouraging other sources of meat to be found from more exotic creatures. Pigeon, whale flesh, and horse meat became unrationed alternatives for the adventurous carnivore. While fish wasn't rationed they were scarce as few fishermen wished to risk sailing far out in the face of submarine attack. The South African snoek (snook) made an appearance in British fishmongers for the first time but was deemed a poor substitute for traditional fishes and largely remained on the shelves despite optimistic recipe suggestions from the MoF (Ministry of Food). At the end of the war snoek was repurposed as 'Selected cuts of fish for cats and kittens'.

The Price of Fish in Yeovil

SIR – Any suspicion of profiteering or of juggling with food supplies has a bearing on the maintenance of civilian morale. The high prices of fish in Yeovil has long been the subject of criticism, but no word of explanation has been forthcoming except the now well-worn excuse 'There's a war on'. Why, for instance are sprats ten-pence a pound in Yeovil when at Dorchester on Saturday they were selling at five-pence and six-pence. It cannot be contended that Yeovil's were a superior brand of sprats nor that freight charges to Yeovil account for the extra.

IMPECUNIOUS

Yeovil, 24th January, 1941

Horses for Courses

SIR – Horses are admirable 'friends of man' in their proper spheres of pulling railway days but on the farms they eat almost as much as they produce. Much of their foodstuff is imported and vital shipping space is taken up. Farmers find that due to war-time limitations they cannot get tractors to help their win-the-war efforts of producing vital food. The Ministry should see that British-made tractors and implements are available by taking off manufacturing restrictions, which are seriously impeding the 'Dig for Victory'.

G. KENNING

Chesterfield, 7th March, 1941

Fishy Prices

SIR – Why is it that shopkeepers are not made to display the price on all their foods? I went into a Cheltenham shop for some rock salmon. After I had been served I inquired the price, and was told 1s. 8d. per pound. When I asked why was it 1s. 6d. in other shops, I was told that it must be a different kind. I was not aware that there were two kinds of rock salmon.

WONDERING

Cheltenham, 21st March, 1941

Fish Should Be Rationed

SIR – We feel that the MoF would be doing a service to the middle and poorer classes if they rationed fish as well as meat. It has become very obvious that the hotels, boarding-houses, and so on, have all their orders put up, and we ordinary housewives have to have what is left, if any—which usually means dried salt cod and, if lucky, herrings or sprats.

The fish shops are now kept closed until all the orders are ready to be delivered. We, the rest of the public, stand waiting and see chickens, rabbits, and fish being loaded up to be delivered to the lucky ones. Where is the equality?

S.E.T

Cheltenham, 15th December, 1941

Need of Fish for Children

SIR – The child's meat ration is half the amount of the adult's. There is no longer a priority from them in eggs. We therefore must rely on an occasional supply of fish. I am sure that many mothers will agree with me that meals are even more of a complication when the family is very small—for instance, one adult and a child under six. One is invariably told, often quite rudely, that there is 'no fish to-day' while inside the shop rows of moist packages topped by dockets, discreetly await the lucky customers who have ordered them. The whole thing makes one feel quite sick when one sees one's toddler go back home to another meal of cheese. I sometimes wonder whether Lord Woolton realises that the creamed liver dishes, the sweetbreads, stewed rabbit (or brains) and creamed herring roes prescribed in the Ministry of Food's leaflet for children's meals, are non-existent in Cheltenham at least.

WELL-WISHER

Cheltenham, 16th December, 1942

Unfair Fish Rationing

SIR – May I voice my protest against the unfair rationing of fish to 'catering establishments'?

It seems ridiculous that hoteliers like myself, who have turned 75 per cent of our accommodation over to the Services and essential workers, are not allowed to buy more than 70 lbs. of fish per month, when the normal consumption previously was, approximately, 300 lbs. per month. On the other hand, 'residential hotels' are permitted to buy any quantity they can obtain. I normally cater for about 40 to 50 guests, and, in addition, non-residents can make use of the hotel for regular meals, and as the ration of meat permitted is 1d. per person per meal, and poultry is almost unobtainable, it seems incredibly unfair that because we open our restaurant to business people we are handicapped.

C. GRAHAME IRVING

Cheltenham, 20th January, 1943

Why Fish and Chips Are Dearer

SIR – Fats have increased in price no less than 72 per cent; coke, 156 per cent; fish, 166 per cent; fillets, 400 per cent. Wages have almost doubled, and staffs increased. At the present moment with very restricted days of opening an eight-week period of fat ration cannot be made to last beyond five weeks, and businesses have to be closed for the remaining three weeks with no saving of the weekly wages bill and overhead. Five weeks' trading must cover a period of eight weeks' expenses. The consumer is not paying unduly for the luxury of a hot supper in these austere days, and judging by the long queues long before opening time, a cooked meal of fish and chips is hardly the last resource of the housewife.

FISH FRYER

Sunderland, 17th November, 1945

Small Fry

SIR – May I draw attention to an injustice now being inflicted on the public by fish and chip shop proprietors. A while ago a pennyworth of chips became twopennyworth overnight. The reason for this (we are told) was an increase in the price of cooking fat of 3d. per lb. This means that a shop using 56lb. of fat a week sold hundreds of portions of chips at a penny extra to cover 14s. extra cost of fat; result a handsome increase in net profits.

SMALL FRY

Leeds, 15th April, 1947

Horse Flesh 'on the Menu'

SIR – In your article on the high rate of horse slaughter there is cause for alarm among those interested in preserving our native breeds of ponies. Has anyone got any information as to how much healthy horseflesh finds its way into shops and into tinned meats for human consumption (unlabelled as horseflesh), and how much finds its way into the black market? What prices are paid for suckling colts for slaughter? The black market alone is responsible for the danger to our meat ration, our horses, and our bird life.

MRS J.D. LOWRY

Plymouth, 15th December, 1947

Mechanised Monster

SIR – As man sends his faithful friend (the horse) to the slaughterhouse, so the great mechanized monster grows and grows. Little does blind and foolish man realise that over-mechanisation is his greatest peril. Sooner or later this evil monster will wreck civilisation.

N. EDWARD HOGGE

Plymouth, 15th December, 1947

Whale Sale

SIR – May I point out to all butchers who have designs on the sale of whalemeat that this commodity is the produce of the work of fishermen, and warrants distribution through the fishing industry? Some remarks have been made about its fishy flavour. This slight fishy-oily taste is not caused through contamination by contact with fish.

H. G

Nottingham, 24th July, 1948

Few Want Snoek

SIR – I read the other day that the housewife can look forward to supplies of tunny and mackerel (canned). Having been initiated into the doubtful delights of *snoek*, informed that I shouldn't know the difference between butter and margarine, one looks forward to a very different handling of our food policy. Speaking as a shopkeeper as well as a housewife, I would state that at no time have I been asked for *snoek*. The cats will have a delightful time varying their menu between the aforementioned three types of fish.

ROSEMARY L. BAKER.

Nottingham, 8th April, 1949

Generation Whale Meat Vitamins Optional

SIR – The present cut in the meat ration impels me to write and ask what this Government, who are so proud of their child welfare schemes, intend to do for the children of two to five years of age. They are too old for priority eggs, but too young for school meals, yet at this age, when they are running around all day, using a tremendous amount of energy they require a full and varied diet to keep them fit.

Are the present rations with 4d of meat plus 1d worth of corned beef supposed to achieve this result? It dismays me to consider what sort of future generation we are bringing up on corned-beef hash or tinned whale meat. It irritates me beyond words when the 'powers that be' prate on about the mothers who fail to collect orange juice and cod liver oil.

OLD MOTHER HUBBARD

Sunderland, 6th April, 1949

12

Sweeter Living

Sugar was one of the first things to be rationed and to the horror of children and adults alike attendant sweet things quickly followed suit. The one succour to the public was a doubling of the sugar ration in the summer months to encourage people to engage in berry picking and jam production. Lacking sugar Brits turned to salt to add some flavour to often tasteless dishes, and jam, which they could use to sweeten the abominable National Loaf.

Sweetie Hoarders

SIR – It was pleasing to note 'Pall Mall's' reference to the retail confectioners regarding hoarding of stocks of sweets.

No doubt these hoarders, and especially those who have closed down shops for the time being, have jumped to the conclusion that the more points they can collect, the more stock they will get.

The wholesale confectioners of Hull have been working in full harmony for a long time now and, with the exception of two, are 100 per cent strong. I am sure that every member of this association, together with most of the retailers in the city, deplore this action on the part of a few.

I implore every shopkeeper to adhere strictly and only to the retaining of 25 per cent of present stocks to July 27, and can assure them that percentage will be able for all needs.

MAURICE KIRMAN

Hull, 20th June, 1942

Ration Cakes?

SIR – I think, as a business person connected with flour confectionery, it would be a good idea to put cakes on a weekly ration. Both the customer and the shopkeeper would be better satisfied.

Workers complain they give up parts of their lunch hour to do shopping and find shops closed. Shops would not be compelled to close if they were not short-staffed.

SMALL BAKER

Preston, 23rd December, 1942

Stealing Candy

SIR – Has anyone ever thought how many pounds of sweets will go into a house with, say, seven or more children from the ages six months to 18 years? Are men and women at 19 children? They never used to be.

No one grudges a child some sweets, but ½ lb. is carrying it too far. The adults used to have the ½ lb., while we kiddies were delighted to have a 1d worth. We were told, as children, that sweeties were bad for our teeth and for giving us spots.

I quite expect a torrent on my head, but you lucky people who walk home with some pounds of sweets, give a thought to the childless folk who carry home their handsome allowance of 3 oz. a week.

OVER EIGHTEEN

Dundee, 25th October, 1944

Sugar Jammed

SIR – There is to be an abundant harvest of wild and

cultivated rasps if the conditions continue favourable. Sugar seems to be abundant.

Your issue of to-day reports that the liner Empire Haig was loading 6000 tons of sugar at Dundee for Rangoon. I wonder if Mr Strachey would help to soothe the temper of our irate womenfolk by increasing the ration of sugar for jam and jelly making at home? Mr Churchill once reduced the price of sugar when he was MP for Dundee. It's a good precedent, Mr Strachey, a real sop to soothe Cerberus and help the inhabitants of Great Britain to eat up their bread ration which seems to be going stale on their hands.

At any rate, it's a pity to see valuable fruit being wasted for the want of sugar.

WILLIAM C. RAMSAY

Dundee, 18th July, 1946

Sweets for German Children

SIR – It has been suggested that the Government should sponsor a scheme whereby those who sign to do so should be allowed to give up part of their sweets ration as a Christmas present to the German children, who are living in such misery in the British zone.

We cannot saddle these little ones with responsibility for the evils of the Nazi regime. Cannot we help in this way to brighten their Christmas?

LESTER SMITH

Hastings and St Leonards, 7th December, 1946

Sugar Starved

SIR – I read with profound disgust this fickle Government's deliberate turning down of a much needed consignment of sugar, their paltry excuse being a shortage of dollar purchasing power. Surely, after a period of eight long years of meagre rations in sugar, the British housewife and her family are entitled to an increase in this much needed commodity.

Why, I ask, should the British people be the sole race, - Germany excepted (and of course they lost the war) –who are still rationed for sugar.

If, as the Government point out, we are in desperate straits, and in consequence have to drastically cut down our imports, why not curtail American films? Also those expensive foreign fruits which are out of reach of the poorer classes. Yes, give us more sugar for goodness sake.

E. U.

Nottingham, 4th June, 1947

Sugar for Blackberries

SIR – At this time of the year with children enjoying long holidays, what can be more profitable and enjoyable for them and parents than to go out into the beautiful sunshine and fresh air picking blackberries? It should be the duty and pleasure of teachers to organize parties for blackberrying combined with Nature study.

Every pound made into jam saves a similar or even larger quantity of imports and double or treble the value in dollars. A saving will be effected in the home, as 2lb. of jam (made from fruit which cost nothing but labour) works out at about 4d., whereas the same quantity of imported jam costs about 1s. 4d. At the present moment millions of blackberries perish for the want of picking, and if they were scarce, millions of people would queue up for them at 2s. 9d. per lb., as they have done this summer for cherries.

W.F. KNIGHT

Plymouth, 2nd September, 1947

Currant Affairs

SIR – I am told that dried fruit (currants in particular) is distributed to retailers according to their sugar registrations. How is it that certain multiple shops which have no sugar registrations can sell the fruit more or less ad lib to the regular queuees, while people who are unable to queue have to go short?

R. BERESFORD

Leeds, 25th November, 1947

Fair Share of Sweets

SIR – Until sweets are as plentiful as they were before the war, rationing should continue, but with a more generous allowance. I well remember the under-the-counter methods until Lord Woolton introduced sweet rationing to enable people to have a fair share.

C.H.

Nottingham, 5th September, 1948

Raspberry

SIR – It is always the thrifty, capable housewife who suffers. When Mr Strachey announced a calamitous cut of 6 lb. sugar per head per annum he should not try to disguise this unpleasant fact by calling it a 'jam bonus' or words to this effect.

CALL A SPADE A SPADE

Dundee, 17th August, 1948

Planned Sweetness

SIR – At last our Minister of Food has been forced to act upon pressure and release some of his huge stocks of sugar.

This pressure has been largely due to the untiring research work during the past months of the Scottish Housewives' Association and which was finally brought to a head during our stormy interview with Mr Strachey in Dundee a few weeks ago.

At that meeting Mr Strachey refused to divulge bulk buying prices on the plea that he was buying at such advantageous prices it would be contrary to our interests in the press it appears this was an erroneous statement as far as sugar is concerned.

He was equally reticent regarding meat prices, and I cannot help feeling that he is being able to cover up much of his price deficiency in bulk buying and administrative costs in food subsidies.

I suggested to Mr Strachey that we poor mortals are undoubtedly the victims of organizations known as 'Planning' and that it is rather a coincidence that a meeting of 'Planning Forum' held only last Wednesday in London should precede our Minister of Food's announcement of a small increase in our rations.

I ask the women of our country to join our association. Let them rise above party politics so that we can pass on an honoured inheritance to our children.

MRS E. M. PATTULLO, SCOTTISH HOUSEWIVES' ASS.

Dundee, 4th November, 1948

Counting Cubes

SIR – In reply to 'One Who Can Count' may I point out that the grocer cannot have 'favourites' when he is supplying sugar. The Food Officer grants permits equivalent to the amount required for registered customers, therefore, there is none to hand out ad. lib., as she suggests. 'One Who Can Count' would be welcomed by the grocer to lend a hand as he is counting all the time.

MONTROSE GROCER

Dundee, 13th November, 1948

Sugar and Soil

SIR – I have read the letter from Mrs Jeannie Mackie. I do not see much connection between our non-existent jam-sugar ration and soil erosion or what Mrs Mackie expects the housewife to do about it.

Mrs Mackie is living on a farm, where she gets all the

milk, eggs, poultry, &c. she can possibly need. It is taking too much on herself to 'threap down the throats' of town dwellers, who have none of these things, that their rations are adequate.

CHARITY BEGINS AT HOME

Dundee, 19th February, 1949

Sugar Ration

SIR – I would like to speak in praise of Lady Riddell-Webster's splendid letter. She rightly says that Mr Strachey said what was 'just not true' when he stated the ration this year would be pounds more than last year. I also took sugar for jam, and in July 1948 had 12 lb. per book and 6 lb. bonus, making 18 lb. This July 2 oz. extra will only give 6 lb. per book and 7 lb. bonus will make only 13 lb., losing 10 lb. of jam per book.

Mr. Strachey also said the great majority of housewives made only a small quantity of jam. This also is just not true. When fruit was allowed to come to the shops in large quantities at a reasonable price, most wives made their jam and saved even off their ordinary ration.

Lady Riddell-Webster suggests that S.W.R.I. might make a distribution if sugar was allowed.

I got sugar in this way myself before this Government came in. We lived in the north of Fife for 40 years and had heaps of fruit, and I got allocations through the local W.R.I. as did every house in the country, big or small, that had fruit and applied. I asked for 30 lb. and got it and later a member came to see the 60 lb. of jam. In the 1914-18 was I also got 30 lb. allocations.

Large numbers of elderly housewives cannot afford to pay the big prices asked for jam.

A. W.

Dundee, 12th March, 1949

Sweet Nightmare

SIR – Surely the Government will not make the mistake with points rationing that they have made with sweets. Let them increase the ration per head for a period before completely de-rationing staple foods.

If they had increased the sweet ration to eight ounces per week for, say, six months, I think all this under-the-counter and queuing nightmare could have been avoided.

MODERATE CONSUMER

Leeds, 27th May, 1949

Share Your Sweeties

SIR – It looks as if sweets are once again to go on the ration. The majority of the public, I am safe to say, would welcome a comeback to rationing and it is also safe for me to assert that the majority of shopkeepers deplore the very idea of a comeback. As for the Ministry of Food, they are simply sweating to have the distribution back on control.

It would mean that more people would receive a fairer share and it would also mean cutting down by more than half these very long sweetie queues.

JOHN PRAIN

Dundee, 30th June, 1949

Sugar Socialism

SIR – Much has been said and written about the sweet ration since this very essential commodity became de-rationed. Some very brainy people have said some very unreasonable things about the shops. This, I think, is most unfair, because shops are only there to buy and sell and serve the community. They were never intended for the elaborate method of rationing. Their turnover does not meet the financing of extra staff, and they just cannot cope.

Only the Ministry of Food can afford the extra staff for this job; they just thrive on it!

But the real point of this matter is—what has happened to the theory of Socialism? We hear plenty of it being professed, but I am afraid there is not much of it being practiced. After all, Socialists should not grab things, they should see that everything is shared. It is only the 'bad old capitalists' who used to grab everything and leave nothing else for the people. So, the people who are buying 10 oz. of sweets every week, just buy 5 oz., and perhaps less, and you will find that the sweets are there all right.

If everybody reduced their consumption by 10 per cent, there would be a surplus of sweets... at least a small, comfortable surplus which would prevent queuing. For my part, I would introduce a bye-law prohibiting queuing in the streets.

RATEPAYER

Dundee, 6th July, 1949

Three Quarters Sweet

SIR – If Mr Reid's statements in to-day's *Courier and Advertiser* are correct about sugar it certainly is high time something was done about it.

Even for medicine we have been strictly rationed on a 75 per cent pre-war consumption basis, and with our increased influx of people to Dundee and the war-time conditions generally we have been hard put to supply the medicines required and ordered by the doctors for both private and insured patients. The harassed housewives who have been kept hunting round after sugar substitutes with absolutely no food value at all will also be interested to know about this glut of sugar in Jamaica.

CHEMIST

Dundee, 15th October, 1949

Jamming

SIR – Housewives who were brought up to consider it bad

housekeeping if they had not enough home-made jam to last them the whole year round are gradually having their pride and skill taken away. The shops are full of jam which many women could have made themselves if the price of the fruit had been reasonable and an adequate amount of sugar available at the right time.

We are still asked to believe that everything is so much better with the Welfare State, but people who want to get things the easy way (jam without the work of making it, for instance) have also been 'feather-bedded' and subsidised as well as the farmer.

FARMER'S WIFE

Dundee, 30th January, 1951

Sweet Scholar

SIR – I admire the courage of 'Confectioner' in advocating not only the de-rationing of sweets but also the removal of price control. He admits that prices would be higher for a time (how nice for confectioners!) but thinks that competition would bring them down. Surely we all know by now that when demand exceeds supply, competition makes prices go up: while, if ever supply overtakes demand, rationing will be abolished as a matter of course.

He is wrong in saying that as long as food is subsidized there will never be de-rationing (except sweets). What about bread?

STUDENT

Bedford, 8th June, 1951

Sugar Economy

SIR – I would be very much obliged if 'Sugar Economy' would let your readers know just how many pounds of jam and marmalade she was able to make last year.

Also how many cakes, puddings, buns, &c., she gets from one pound of sugar.

I take no sugar in my tea, and I had to borrow to get 10 pounds of sugar for my marmalade, and I shall have to repay it at half a pound per week. I cannot think her children get the daily amount of sugar they ought to have, even with syrup. 'Sugar Economy' does not mention using honey.

I realize that sugar is a vital item of export for us or I would be initiating a vigorous campaign for the immediate derationing of sugar.

J. I. R.

Dundee, 25th February, 1953

Sugar for Toffee

SIR – Mr Butler has said sugar was soon to be derationed. Why does he not take brown sugar off the ration and let the housewife get some good home made toffee, as in the good old days.

JEAN MASSON

Dundee, 18th April, 1953

100 per cent Fruit Jam

SIR – The article by your farming reporter calls for comment. Before me lies the minute-book of the Agricultural and Rural Housing Committee, S.W.R.I., and the following is an excerpt from minutes of a meeting held on May 30, 1952: 'In view of the heavy fruit crop, and in order to bring on the markets an improved article of food, the delegates unanimously agreed that the Minister of Food be asked to raise the standard of jam to 50 per cent fruit, 50 per cent sugar, thus making it equal to homemade jam.'

Regarding Whitehall trying to persuade women that jam 'must' contain 60 per cent sugar, the reverse was the case, and we do not forget the waste arising from following their advice in early war years, when we tried to make do with ¾ pound sugar to 1 pound fruit. We have long since gone back to the method which has stood the test of time—pound for pound.

And an important point, housewives make their jam for their own households, manufacturing for sale is quite a different story.

MARGARET FLETCHER

Dundee, 21st March, 1953

13

Light and Coal

Britain's streets were a dangerous place to be under the blackouts even if one wasn't under the threat of air-raids. Road accidents skyrocketed despite the 20mph speed limit. Light and heat were in short supply with coal rations and restrictions on the use of electricity in town and at home. Petrol was rationed, prohibiting 'joy rides' and limiting private travel unrelated to business or necessity. Instead buses, and bus queues became the order of the day. Britain was a cold, damp, dark and isolated place in winter.

Coal Cuts

SIR – The Ministry of Mines has hastily introduced the rationing of coal at 2cwt. per week.

The coal shortage is not real but artificial, and it is high time the responsibility for this muddle was placed upon the proper shoulders. The Ministry of Transport last month authorised prohibitive charges on wagons making it impossible for the merchants to hold reserve stocks for emergencies.

MERCHANT

Leeds, 2nd February, 1940

Light-Up

SIR – I suggest that it should be made compulsory for every

householder to whiten the kerb outside his house and the kerb of any carriage-way into his premises. A standard width could be arranged, and the individual cost would be very little. Many accidents in the black-out are caused through people tripping over an invisible kerb, and one can get a nasty jolt when walking alone the centre of the pavement and suddenly stepping off the kerb of a carriage entrance.

CHARLES J. H. MCREA

Berwick upon Tweed, 8th February, 1940

Stamp for Petrol

SIR – We have now to apply twice to two separate departments for petrol. This means 5d. in stamps, two lots of paper and two envelopes. A Government Department is wasting paper and public funds.

LEONARD SMITH

Leeds, 11th May, 1940

Chinks in the Black-Out

SIR – Wood screens, as suggested by Mr Ross, are certainly the only efficient method of blacking out a window, but I wonder if he realises the difficulty in getting the wood to make them just now. Any sort of wood won't do. It has to be clear of knots, or the frame will twist or break over by a knot. And the cost is rather prohibitive now owing to a 100% increase in price in the cost of wood as from September 1.

Experience has taught us that any material that is a dead black-out won't run on a blind roller, and any material that will run on a blind roller is not sufficiently dense to be a black-out.

Holland linen blinds show a glare through them, and any blind fitted on a roller between the window frame is bound to show light at the sides, as space has to be left for working the blinds at the sides. Some windows have enough space on the woodwork inside to fix the blind to cover the full width of the window, but in the majority of cases there isn't room enough for the blind roller fittings to be fixed.

Another method is a roller fixed to the bottom of a blind, covering the full width of the window on the inside, and made to roll up by two cords fixed from top of window, round roller and up again through two pulleys at the top. In this case the roller winds the blind up from the bottom. This method has proved very efficient in difficult cases.

My sympathy goes out to the owners of steel windows with handles and ventilator rods jutting out in the room, and very little margin at the sides of windows. In their case nothing can be done on the window. It is a case for curtains.

In connection with curtains, we are very unfortunate again, as at the moment not an inch of a famous and efficient curtain rail can be got, even if you were prepared to pay double the price for it.

My experience is that most people are more apprehensive of a visit from the people re their lights than they are of Hitler and his air gangsters.

JOINER

Dundee, 25th November, 1940

Black Out Offenders

SIR – Air raid wardens have no power to deal with black-out offenders. Such powers are in the hands of the police and special constabulary. Air raid wardens should therefore not be blamed for any possible breach in the black-out regulations.

AIR-RAID WARDEN

Barnstaple, 17th October, 1940

Waster Current

SIR – During these days we are asked to avoid waste in every shape and form, and I venture to suggest that our Corporation could set a very fine example by not using the new twilight system of street lighting on bright moonlight evenings. I realise that we purchase the current in bulk and possibly on contract, but that hardly justifies us wasting it.

FIRE-WATCHER

Cheltenham, 21st March, 1941

Fresh-Air

SIR – My son, who was in the first group conscribed into the mines and has spent over three years at the coal-face. He was taken from farming, and is fully prepared to work seven days a week, at half the wages, and exist on present rations, for the privilege of working in God's fresh air. I would ask your correspondent to ask themselves 'Would I change my job for that of a miner?' Otherwise, the outlook for the whole community will be bleak indeed.

A.F.D.

Leeds, 21st March, 1942

Lights Out

SIR – In considering rationing of light has anyone given thought to the many thousands of users of electric light, who only found it possible to have it installed on the prepayment system of wiring? If we are to use only 80 per cent. of last year's total it will be 80 per cent. of what? The actual current used, or the meter reading, which includes repayment? Perhaps the Electricity Committee might be interested enough to inquire whether this supposition is correct and delve deeper into it.

PROBABLE VICTIM

Lincoln, 13th May, 1942

Gas Guzzling Shakespeare

SIR – I am one of those numerous motorists whose basic ration ceases at the end of this month and who were informed that shortage of supplies of petrol, shortage of shipping for its import, increasing requirements of our fighting services, and curtailment of mere pleasure-seeking, made the restrictment necessary. It rather jars, therefore, to see an advertisement of a Shakespeare play at Kemnay to which special buses are to be run from Aberdeen, a distance of fifteen miles either way. Is this not pleasure seeking and is it for this our sacrifice is being made?

FAIR PLAY

Aberdeen, 23rd June, 1942

Manager's Petrol

SIR – I personally travel the Midlands on work of first class priority, and my shortest journey must be logged. Why not the executives?

EX-ROYAL NAVY SUBMARINE SERVICE

Cheltenham, 16th December, 1942

Shopping Cars

SIR – I should like to ask why so many use their cars for shopping and get away with it. Evidently they hold a permit for their journey to work. But the petrol allowance runs to all this waste and misuse. It is irritating to those who are sacrificing so much to see this wanton waste and indifference to the war effort. Cannot the local Petroleum Officer stop the surplus petrol and this 'one-sided' use of cars?

A. SADLER

Cheltenham, 16th December, 1942

Convoy Comfort

SIR – My husband has been convoying since 1939, and not once at Cosham have I had any difficulty in getting any of his rations. The grocer has always found him an egg, the butcher always the meat, and we always had extra milk. Also, we went to a little mining village at the end of at the end of 1941 for a week outside of Barnsley. The shopkeepers could not do enough for my husband. At that time there was a terrible cigarette shortage there, but I was told my husband could have as many as he wanted. The miners were rationed, and as most of them chew tobacco in the pits to stop the coal dust in their throats, it hit them hard, so I promptly bought all I could get hold of and sold them to the miners. May I add, and my husband agrees, I'd rather him convoying than be a miner. I can only say I've only admiration for the miners and their wives, and we in the South are lucky to get our rations, when we like, compared to miners' wives once a week.

A COSHAM RESIDENT

Portsmouth, 28th July, 1943

Still We Shiver

SIR – Many thousands of people in this country would like to share in Mr. Shinwell's optimism regarding the nationalisation of the mines. Does he base his optimism on the belief that when the mines are nationalised there will be no more absenteeism? I wonder how Mr. Shinwell would like to have to manage on two cwt. for December, January or February.

W. B. BOLLAND

Cheltenham, 14th December, 1945

Bit the Dust

SIR – The cut in the food rations did not come as a surprise, and one wonders what influential effect Ernest Bevin and Co. had in maintaining the rations as we did. Let us compare the 'private hotels and restaurants of London,' revelling in abundance of such things, for those who have money to burn, and the Snowdown miner and surface worker with more than their ration of coal dust in the course of their employment, in their endeavour to maintain output to keep body and soul together. The lack of such 'fats' so essential to the human body may be the cause of sickness and a C3 race.

ANDREW R. MCKNIGHT

Dover, 1st June, 1945

Cycling Risks

SIR – The basic petrol ration has been restored and the further relaxation of petrol rationing is being spoken of. The return of cars to the roads has been allowed without the return of driving tests. These conditions will increase the already alarmingly high road accident figures. Educational Authorities should be urged to provide road safety lessons as part of educational training.

A. A. G. SWALES, BEDFORD ROAD CYCLING CLUB

Bedford, 27th July, 1945

September Is the Cruellest Month

SIR – On October 1 I applied at the Post Office for my basic petrol ration, and I was handed a ration book from September to February. The September coupons were torn out. Surely 12 months' licence should entitle me to 12 month's basic ration. I shall be grateful, indeed, for some clarification of this muddle.

G. E. A. ROSLYN

Lincoln, 4th October, 1945

Pay Per Mile

SIR – The only really equitable system of petrol rationing is by mileage, and certainly not by a flat rate. In South Africa during the war we were limited to 200 miles per month (no single journey in any car to be longer than 72 miles). Our car, which does 18 miles to the gallon, would get 11 gallons on the South African system, while my neighbour's 10 h.p. car, capable of 37 miles to the gallon, would get 5 ½ gallons. Under the present scheme the most I can hope for is about

320 miles per month, while my neighbour's 10 h.p. car does 444.

P. SHAW JEFFREY

Leeds, 25th July, 1946

Where Does the Coal Go?

SIR – It is all very well for the Government to keep telling us our coal output is rising, but where on earth does it rise to? If we are now increasing the output how is it we see about one bag in four to six weeks, when during the war we were getting our full ration?

BRIQUETTE

Leeds, 10th March, 1947

Why Spite the Motorist?

SIR – The motorists falls in the class which does not matter a tinker's cuss. Motorists are already in possession of basic ration coupons from October to February. A week or so ago we were told that there would be a cut of 33½ per cent. Now we are told that it is all off. This Government is clawing the air like some demented lunatic. It is not the fault of the motorist the miner will not work, that they are downing tools on the slightest occasion that they believe because the mines are under Government control there is no longer any need to work.

There are 11,000,000 who voted anti-Socialist. It is about time we told them where to get off.

W. EDWARDS

Plymouth, 2nd September, 1947

Coal Hole

SIR – I live in a flat, and when I tipped my coalman for carrying my bags up the steps all was in order. One day the coal came when I was at business and the next time I saw the coalman he said 'You haven't given me anything for last time. You can carry it up yourself in future'. I saw the boss, but got no satisfaction, so I sent a registered letter to the Ministry of Fuel and Power in London. They sent a man to investigate. The answer was, 'The man won't carry the coal up in case he hurts himself. Who is going to pay compensation?' Do they expect the women who also live in our flats to carry their coal up?

CONCERNED

Leeds, 25th November, 1947

Gestapo

SIR – Within a week of the end of 'free' motoring, some persons appear to have taken on the task of gestapo agents. Before reporting the suspecting erring motorist may I suggest that these ardent persons make sure of one of two facts, namely; (1) Is the motorist's stopping place a 'permitted' destination or (2) Is the stopping place on a permitted route. They would probably save the police and themselves unnecessary work and the motorists, considerable annoyance. –

SNOOPER'S VICTIM

Yeovil, 12th December, 1947

Unsporting Petrol

SIR – While we poor private motorists are kept off the road through the withdrawal of the basic petrol ration, hundreds of buses are travelling every Saturday conveying football fans hundreds of miles. For the Rugby international between Scotland and Wales at Cardiff last Saturday, a party travelled the long distance from Galashiels. Where does the saving of petrol come in when this is allowed?

MOTORIST

Berwick upon Tweed, 17th February, 1948

Petrol Peculiarities

SIR – The injustice of the new basic petrol allowance is simply an extension of a policy of injustices which has existed for a long while at the Ministry of Fuel. I am one of the 16 representatives that my company employs whose duties are entirely advising and selling machinery, for plant maintenance purposes, from farms to coal mines, from gas works to textile manufacturers. Each representative has the same job to do and on the question of mileage there is very little difference in their territories. Yet not one of the 16 representatives has the same allocation of units. Some have 'E' units, some have 'S' units, and the amount of petrol is different in each case.

We hesitate to draw comparisons with our better-treated colleagues, fearing lest, by so doing, the levelling instinct of the civil servant will operate to our colleagues' disadvantage. Those who are most generously treated were able to run their cars during the war years and since the war have had their allowance improved. The men with the smaller allowance are ex-Servicemen. It means for some part of the next six months I shall be out of work, I have a wife and three children to keep and I have rent to pay and food to buy.

C. F. WHEELER

Derby, 12th May, 1948

Shy Mince

SIR – May I call the attention of the powers that be to the state of the pit canteens? As far as cleanliness is concerned there is much to be desired, the food is poor and there is waste through food being spoiled by bad cooking. Many a time a shift comes off to dins there is nothing to be got. How can this happen? A fair estimate of what is called a dinner is a plate of soggy potatoes and half-cooked cabbage swimming in some greasy concoction misnamed gravy. And somewhere hidden from view, too shy to show itself, is a piece of meat, or mincemeat. How coal can be produced under these conditions beats me.

SUFFERER

Sunderland, 18th November, 1948

Perfidious Petrol

SIR – With references to petrol rationing, it is the unfairness of distribution that is so exasperating. While one businessman ridicules the idea of 'saving up' owing to his small ration, I know another business man who not only has sufficient petrol to permit him to use his car over double the standard 'basic' distance of 90 miles a month—using unfairly his business allowance—but has coupons to spare and return at the end of the period. It is obvious that the above case is only one of many.

DISSATISFIED

Leeds, 17th January, 1949

Rationing by Overcharge

SIR – When the British Electricity Authority made known its intention to ration the supply of current by a system of overcharging for the winter quarter's supply, it was careful to infer that reduced charges for the three remaining quarters would compensate for the winter overcharge if due economy was exercised in the consumption of current. Application of the new rates just imposed show that the current consumed in the winter quarter would have to be less than the average of the combined three remaining quarters an amount equal to more than three times the consumption of the winter quarter! It is quite clear that few, if any, consumers will avoid an overcharge on the year's consumption. I have sent an objection on the method of imposing this further increase, following a 50 per cent increase which was imposed in June, 1948, especially as it is not applied to consumers with slot-meter supplies.

CHARLES E. BANKS

Redhill, 18th March, 1949

Stung

SIR – I am in complete agreement with Mr. Bank's letter, but I do not think he can possibly mean what he infers by his reference to 'slot meter supplies.' If he is afraid that this overcharge will be used to subsidise the 'slot meter' customers, please let me put my case. In February my meter gave up £2 19s. to the collector for current used during the winter quarter. This heavy traffic of coin through the slot took its toll of the meter's mechanism, and a new meter was installed on March 2nd, and up to March 21st, seventeen of my hard-earned 'bobs' had been fed into it, and Mr. Banks must remember this does not supply electricity to a whole house. Being only a sub-tenant, I can do nothing to obtain my electricity at a cheaper rate.

SOUTH MERSTHAM

Redhill, 25th March, 1949

Punitive Petrol

SIR – Regarding this iniquitous 9d on petrol, which rations it more severely than when we had 'basic' would it not have been a workable plan to let motorists decide whether to remain on 'basic' and pay half the licence or to be derationed and have to pay the full amount?

In the case of those who only use a car for necessity in a country district (where no bus is available) and do not go long joy-rides, surely this scheme would be appropriate.

Also, it is most unfair that an old car, say, of 9 h.p., is taxed twice the size and power.

OLDMELDRUM

Aberdeen, 26th June, 1950

A Lochee Black-Out

SIR – Tonight we in this part of Lochee had what I suppose is called a sectional electrical black-out which must have lasted the best part of an hour. When the electricity department belonged to the town this would have been rectified in a very short time. Now that electricity has been nationalised, I understand the Hydro-Electric Board has to fig out some employee in Broughty Ferry and instruct him to see to the matter. This naturally takes time, and meantime everyone in the section affected is sitting in the dark. Is this the best service we can expect under nationalisation?

GROPING IN THE DARK

Dundee, 4th April, 1952

14

Hitler's Secret Weapon

While not rationed during the war bread was subject to strict controls. Bread had to be made from National Flour. Resembling a greyish sludge with its bran left in National Flour was an unappealing ingredient to work with. Some housewives, exasperated with its stodginess, would sieve the flour through their stockings in an attempt to get white flour. Those who kept chickens would extract the bran from the flour to make a kind of mash as chicken feed.

Britain's National Flour produced the National Loaf, loathed for its taste but universally consumed for its nutrition. Christened 'Hitler's Secret Weapon' for its dreadful taste the National Loaf was successfully produced in such abundance that it didn't need to be rationed. Paradoxically after the war's end bread was rationed as it was alleged people were consuming one of the few unrationed foods at 'immoderate' levels impairing Britain's ability to feed Europe. Bread rationing caused consternation and outrage amongst bakers and housewives alike.

Even a Little Gumption

SIR – May I call to attention for a second time to bread wasting? I noticed on Saturday a quantity of bread in our nearby pig food bin. There were some biggish chunks, and also some very thick slices, with margarine on. I called two persons who were near to see it, and no doubt they would corroborate this statement. Surely the buyers could gauge their bread requirements better by using even a little gumption. At a time like this, when our brave sailors are risking all they have, it makes one both ashamed and indignant at this shameless waste of food.

INDIGNANT

Cheltenham, 10th September, 1942

Mental Compunction

SIR – Bread is to be rationed, making less bread than ever to be shared out. I've got a little inside information from London that tea may come off the ration at the same time as bread is rationed, but it is no use giving with one hand and taking away with the other. If bread is to be rationed there must be stocks against requirements, and if a nation adopts rationing it commits itself and must fulfil its contract as between the State and the people. Let us keep off rationing to the last crumb. France faces financial ruin through rationing and black marketing.

T. R. H.

Hartlepool, 25th June, 1946

Breadtopia

SIR – According to Mr Tom Cook's speech in Dundee last night, 'bread rationing was almost a certainty but he did not think any individual would buy the full quota of bread which would be allowed them.' It would seem that we are to get more bread than we need and than we are at present eating. If so why ration bread at all? The only sense is more controls and coupons for everything and a snooper in every dust bin. Where is this madness to stop?

PUZZLED

Dundee, 26th June, 1946

Labour Supporters Stunned by Bread Rationing

SIR – I am simply an English housewife, content to work for the well-being of my home and family and for the benefit of the community in general, but somehow that desire to work is thwarted by present-day difficulties and responsibilities. I know there are many other women who share my feelings. The news that bread and flour are to be rationed has completely stunned us. I feel sure that we all wish to do all we can to alleviate the sufferings of those starving in Europe, but we must consider our own husbands and children first.

BARBARA J. TOOGOOD

Cheltenham, 2nd July, 1946

Hullabaloo about Bread

SIR – Why all the hullabaloo about bread rationing? Surely the fact that many tons of bread have been collected weekly from the waste or pig bins shows that people have had too much up to now. I know that everybody does not waste bread, but the wasters make conditions worse for the non-wasters.

Is it not rather late in the day to be so concerned about the poor housewife? Hasn't she had to queue for necessities long enough to have got used to it? And isn't she a very tolerant person to have done so quietly when she so often waited outside in the cold for what might be left of fish, meat, cakes and any other ting in short supply, while 'orders' were being put up, to be duly carried to other customers in vans? Many times she had to go away empty-handed.

Some housewives have enough imagination to hear underneath it all the old wolf-cry, 'I'll huff and I'll puff and I'll blow your house in'.

ANTI-BUNK

Cheltenham, 2nd July, 1946

Reasonable Warsight

SIR – We would like to point out that the resolution drawn up by the Women Conservatives of East Surrey is: 'It is the Government's short-sightedness which has brought about the necessity for bread rationing. Had reasonable measures been taken in time this necessity would not have arisen, and we would still be in a position to help other countries. Starvation and misery abroad are not excuses for muddle and inefficiency at home, though they are now often made to serve as such.'

VIOLET FORD

Redhill, 12th July, 1946

Unhappy Lot

SIR – Judging from the correspondence in the *Courier and Advertiser* nobody seems to have a word to say in favour of bread rationing in spite of Mr Strachey's best efforts to convince them in his speech to the Commons last week. According to the official American reports bumper harvests are expected both in that country and in Europe, and there is still a wheat reserve of 11,000,000 tons. Bread rationing therefore at the very worst could only be necessary until the end of August, but once on it will stay on like the coal ration. Fortunately there are to be more dried eggs, and there is word of more meat and butter from Ireland, which, like Denmark and all the other food-producing countries, is dying to sell to us. Will Mr Strachey really try to get more? There is also the possibility of more fats from our East African Colonies, which in normal times export large quantities for soap manufacture. The housewife's lot is indeed not a happy one. She will know all about it during the winter when there is no coal in the bunker and no food in the pantry and an epidemic of influenza raging.

FIFER

Dundee, 16th July, 1946

Master Bakers

SIR – Women know full well that fundamentally rationing is

the only insurance of fair distribution. Lower food prices are required generally, and not increased prices, favoured by the Master Bakers, one suggesting that the saving would be brought about by making the loaf 1/6. More control is called for in this case rather than less.

We are told there is no need for rationing bread, etc., according to the Master Bakers there is plenty available. What then are the queues we see daily, and mainly outside bakers' shops?

ANONYMOUS

Cheltenham, 17th July, 1946

Bread's Darkest Hour

SIR – In view of the decision to put bread and cakes on the ration I think it is indeed time the shopkeeper protested most strongly. Acting as unpaid, unthanked civil servant takes up much of our time already, and if any more restriction, rules and regulations are forced upon us it will be absolutely unbearable, especially after six weary years of war. Although not a Conservative personally, I must agree that Mr. Churchill hit the nail right on the head in recalling that even in the darkest hour of the war when submarine warfare was at its height, it was not necessary to ration bread.

NOBBY

Nottingham, 19th July, 1946

Bakers of Bristol

SIR – The bakers of Bristol refuse to work the bread rationing scheme, and they are instantly threatened with fine and imprisonment. Yet the Government could let the dock strike, which must have cost the country millions of pounds, run on for weeks!

NON-MANUAL WORKER

Nottingham, 19th July, 1946

Starving Germans

SIR – On 12th July I attended a meeting at the Corn Exchange, Bedford, at which T. C. Skeffington-Lodge MP was to speak on Bread Rationing. After his address questions were asked for. When I stood up to ask my question, I was not allowed to put it, but Mr. Skeffington-Lodge said he would see me after the meeting. When I went up on to the platform afterwards, he avoided me so I hope I may ask that question now.

No figures were given by Mr. Skeffington-Lodge as to why bread rationing was necessary. It may be so—I cannot say—but the only reasons given were the starving Germans and the weather.

I would suggest that, if 200,000 tons of Canadian wheat sold to Great Britain at a specially cheap rate and diverted to Europe had been retained by us, if the twelve million tons of wheat which Mr. Eden pointed out in the House was unaccounted for had not been lost and if planning and foresight had been used by the Government, bread rationing would not have been necessary. I therefore ask Mr. Skeffington-Lodge whether he will admit that bread rationing has been brought about through the utter incompetency of the Government?

C. A. A. HIATT (MAJOR)

Bedford, 19th July, 1946

Sharp Loaves

SIR – My question at the Corn Exchange bread meeting was not answered by Mr. Skeffington-Lodge. The loaf was reduced in weight by ¼lb, which is one-eighth of a large loaf. Why has the cash value of this reduction in weight not been passed on to the public? This reduction in weight has reduced the value of a £1 note by 12½ per cent, for to-day we are paying 22s. 6d. for £1's worth of bread.

As to milk, why is it rationed when the production is greater than ever? The wars in Europe and the Far East have been over for a year.

MABEL CHAMBERLAIN

Bedford, 19th July, 1946

Regrettable Necessity

SIR – The decision of the Government to ration bread is the subject of much discussion by the public, and the attitude of bakers to this decision is of no little importance. The Management Committee of the Aylesbury Co-operative Society adheres to the co-operative principle that whatever goods are in short supply should be equitably distributed by rationing, and they therefore feel it incumbent upon them not to be associated with any demonstrations or petitions against bread rationing.

J. E. SAUNDERS

Aylesbury, 19th July, 1946

Indian Bread

SIR – Your correspondent, D. Llewellyn, complaining about bread rationing, takes an appallingly insular view when he grumbles about not being allowed to send food home from India—of all places! In India the winter rains failed and 130 million of its inhabitants are rationed for food grains (rice, wheat, and millet). The average villager depends almost entirely on his grain ration, which, at 12 ozs., gives him 1,200 calories daily—a starvation allowance. In some places the ration is only 7 ozs., and is often not distributed for weeks at a time. Some farm labourers do not get ration cards, as they are supposed to be paid in kind, but their employers are paying them in money, and keeping the food. There is no food to buy without ration cards. The worst period is yet to come; it will be the greatest famine for 50 years unless food is imported on a large scale. I have yet to hear a constructive criticism of bread rationing.

K. FRENCH,

Cheltenham, 19th July, 1946

Dread Bread

SIR – Before coming to the outer island of North Uist as a visitor I dreaded the prospect of a bread, flour, and oatmeal rationing. Now I am here I find all my fears were groundless. The far-seeing, second-sighted natives have generally anticipated the flour and meal restrictions by obtaining sufficient supplies to last until Christmas at least.

I asked one old, weather-beaten crofter's wife what she was going to do with her bread units. She replied, 'Ach, they've not started yet!' With plenty of milk, butter, eggs, crowdie, and fish, they live their simple, happy lives in a land which has never known the queue.

MISS B. MACLEAN

Dundee, 4th August, 1946

Let Them Eat Cream Buns

SIR – 'Banovallum' is only speaking for herself and her friends. Some people eat more than others, and cream buns are no good to a hungry person. The bread rationing is not fair. Some of us would like less sugar and more cheese, but we are not allowed to change. It is bad enough going hungry when you have no money. When you can afford a good plain meal it's a farce. I do not know what some of us would do if the cafes and snack bars were to close.

D. M. LILLBURN (Miss)

Lincoln, 22nd August, 1946

Bread Unit Cornucopia

SIR – I am one of a household of two people. We decided to try this experiment for the first period:

a 3lb. bag of flour for cooking purposes—9 BUs [Bread Units].

one cake—2 BUs.

bread to be eaten at breakfast and tea only.

The flour was exhausted by beginning of the fourth week of the period; the cake was spun out for nearly a fortnight, by which time it showed marked signs of age; the bread gave out with Thursday breakfast in the last week, and but for the kindness of neighbours we should have had to go without until the baker opened on the Monday.

In conversation with other two- and three-person households we found their experience to be much the same, and the second period added confirmation to the opinion that the small household were being rationed with undue severity. On the other hand, the larger households had more BUs than they could use.

Then came the astounding decision of the Food Minister that unwanted BUs could be exchanged. But why? The holders of unwanted BUs had no grievance; they had more bread than they could use. Why then were not surplus B.U.s declared valueless like unused points? The decision is an utter negation of that equality which the whole rationing system of the country was designed to secure. The reason is obvious.

SMALL HOUSEHOLD

Hastings and St Leonards, 28th September, 1946

Omniscient Government

SIR – Mr. Strachey, who rejected with superior wisdom and threats the advice and offered help of the bakers, now, as a result, finds himself in difficulties regarding points, food, good, etc. In his dilemma, and to save his face, he now appeals for the help of the bakers and grocers. This is another instance, among many, of the inept administration and disastrous policy of the Government. What need is there for Mr. Strachey to ask ignorant bakers and grocers for their help and advice?

F. ROBERTS STANNARD

Leeds, 14th October, 1946

15

Christmas Cheer

A rationed Christmas seems antithetical to the consumerist extravaganza that Christmas has come to be and in post-war Britain Christmas seemed to ram home the dull privations of rationing. Nuts, oranges, sweets, warmth and goodwill to all men were in short supply. To add insult to injury the Christmas holidays made it a necessity to stockpile one's rations as the shops shut. Cries for jollity matched those of disappointment at the token ration increase at Christmas.

Cheltenham Locusts

SIR – Personally I am not really interested whether the races are held or not. Most racegoers bring their own lunch-baskets or sandwiches, or so they say. If that is the case, why does a well-known firm cater for luncheons and teas? Our local people know what happened at last Christmas time, when there was influx of visitors to the town. The same thing would occur if the races were held as some people would no doubt stay the two days. The main objection is that the people locally are thinking of their rations, and do not want a repetition of Christmas.

ANOTHER SPORTSMAN

Cheltenham, 5th February, 1941

Paper Planes

SIR – Women who spare a thought for salvage amid all the excitement will be able to do a very good piece of war work, because at no time does so much, useful material come into the average household as at Christmas. Bones from meat and poultry, kitchen waste, paper and string from parcels, will be at a maximum and all are valuable to the war effort. You probably know by heart what purposes they serve: the bones make explosives, oil, glue, and fertilizer; the kitchen waste feeds livestock and poultry; the paper makes shell containers, cartridge boxes, and even aeroplanes, and the string becomes charts and maps, or perhaps felt.

Clean and untorn brown paper, however, should not be sent for salvage, but folded and put away for further us. That is 'indirect salvage' because it saves us from having to make new brown paper.

MARGARET DALEY, AMY WILLIAMS

Portsmouth, 23rd December, 1943

Christmas Oranges

SIR – I read with interest your report of the fruit and potato merchants' annual dinner and 'bowls of oranges and apples'. Twelve days to Christmas, and still no sign of oranges for this area. Perhaps someone could enlighten me as to how this system of fruit distribution works.

We were recently told on the radio 'People should now be getting their second allocation Christmas oranges'. It is three months since I had oranges for my children. During the 'fruit harvest' London's shops were glutted with fruit, while in the South-West the supply was almost nil. Now London gets priority for oranges, and still we get nothing, and no one seems to be interested.

S. SOWDEN

Plymouth, 14th December, 1945

Austerity at New Year Ball

SIR – Imagine my surprise on making my application for tickets for the first peace-time Hospital Ball, when I was informed that there is to be no bar after 10 p.m. Not only is this the case, but I am also informed that despite the Ball continuing until 1 a.m. on New Year's Day, the buffet also has to close at 11 p.m. There must be no alcoholic drink to celebrate the advent of 1946, and not even will a cup of tea or coffee be available to those worthy souls who patronise this dance organised in aid of our local hospitals. Is it not time that we woke up in Cheltenham and reverted to the pre-war days.

WOULD-BE REVELLER

Cheltenham, 14th December, 1945

Brighten an Austerity Christmas

SIR – With 1947 not very far away, is there not something we can do for the children of this town, just to brighten their lives and to give them, at least one cheerful memory of 1946?

Come on you new Councillors, help give the children some fun. Put every other one of those street lights out from Saturday December 21 until Saturday December 28, and with the fuel saved give all shops permission to put as many lights in their shop windows as they wish, preferably coloured lights. How about having four large Christmas trees planted on each corner of the Memorial decorate with coloured lights? I am sure that not only the children, but we 'older children' will really enjoy seeing this poor old town looking cheerful for a few days; and who knows, perhaps it will be the start of a brighter New Year.

VICTOR H. PEARSON

Hastings and St Leonards, 7th December, 1946

Trees Expensive

SIR – Can anyone explain the high prices of Christmas trees?

I have had to pay 12s 6d for one 4½ft. high, or else disappoint my child. It does not seem to be the fault of the retailers. Surely Christmas trees, and, in the same category toys, can hardly be regarded as luxury goods, but as part of a child's normal life?

DONALD B. SHAW

Hull, 20th December, 1946

Goose Fair Food Restrictions

SIR – Nottingham is celebrating its first peace-time Goose Fair for seven years, and the Markets and Fairs Committee invite the people to enter into this celebration in the good old fashioned way. The Ministry of Food, however, has issued an order, to the effect: 'Yes, celebrate if you will, but we shall not allow you to partake of any refreshment, unless you take it to the Fair out of your own rations'. Holidays at home have become a prominent feature of the national life.

F.A. WILLETT

Nottingham, 4th June, 1947

Toy Tractors

SIR – Many Christmas toys for boys are of a warlike nature, guns, tanks, soldiers and son on, thereby encouraging them in marital spirit. I suggest it would be of much greater good to the country if the type of toy were changed to engines, agricultural tractors and implements, working models of miners and similar constructive things. This should help to plant the right outlook on the future.

T. L. BRADLEY

Hull, 15th November, 1947

Tax on Toys

SIR – I expect that everyone in the country feels the same way as I do about this iniquitous tax on children's toys and other children's things which bear such tax. This Socialist Government which is supposed to be the 'workers' Government, seems to be doing all it possibly can to legislate against the class which they are supposed to represent. The previous tax of one third on children's toys was in my opinion deplorable, but now that the tax has gone up to 50 per cent how on earth are parents with modest incomes going to be able to afford, particularly where they have a number of children, to provide toys from them with such Purchase Tax?

I would have preferred, if it was considered essential, to pay 1d or 2d more for my glass of beer than have the children suffer.

(COUN.) P. VERNEY

Hull, 15th November, 1947

No Coal in Stocking

SIR – Many people grumble at being without coal for a few weeks; but I have had no coal or logs since before Christmas. I have no radiator, no oil for cooking stove and no other means whatever for cooking my meals. I go out to almost all my meals, including breakfast. I have sent in two permits allowed me, but nothing has been done yet.

ROUNDHAY

Leeds, 15th April, 1947

High Price of Nuts

SIR – The nut buyer who offered the ridiculous prices of 7s. per lb. stands self-accused. Who, if not he and his fellow-bidders created that particular 'black market'? By so doing he made it impossible for sensible, ordinary people to buy the nuts they would have so much liked to have had for Christmas. The public at last had the good sense to prefer to go without—a really cheering thought.

CHAGFORD

Plymouth, 8th January, 1948

Criminal Colonel Magistrate

SIR – Colonel Ernest Mervyn Joseph of Billericay, Essex, was fined £2 and ordered to pay costs for stealing a Christmas tree, valued at 4s 6d. from the Elvetham Estates. Colonel Joseph in a letter to the court, drew attention to a statement to the police in which he said he thought the estates were a public wood. In the statement he said he came from Colombo Ceylon, where he was a magistrate.

ANONYMOUS

Leeds, 6th September, 1948

Christmas Porkies

SIR – Mr. Strachey says there will be a double ration of meats for sausages and pies for Christmas, but our present allocation of meats is only a third of what is has been other years. I feel sorry for the people who think there will be pies at Christmas.

PORK PIE MAKER

Leeds, 27th November, 1948

Do They Know It's Christmas

SIR – We were better fed during the war than we are now. Rations last about four fays if all meals are taken at home. Talking of the days of 40 or 50 years ago, I didn't know what margarine was then, or foreign meat. Young people now have never known the joys of Christmas, with the well-stocked pantry, turkeys, Christmas puddings with whisky poured on and a match applied to light it up, Christmas trees hanging with bundles of chocolate, and all the good things that are a delight.

K. PLACKETT

Nottingham, 6th December, 1948

Bungled Christmas

SIR – I wonder if the people in charge of our meagre food rations realise what Christmas 1948 will be like for those who have one book to get food, during the four days the shops will be shut. It is sure and certain that the meat will not last four days, and you could expect to get fish to last that time, if you could get it. Even now some shops are sold out before noon.

It will be one egg, cheese at the most to last twice, no tinned meat, salmon, or sardines, and no bacon. I am writing on behalf of elderly people who have the bare ration, and nothing much can be got on points. Nuts and oranges are all very well, but what we all want—and, in fact, badly need—is at least one good meal per day. As it is someone has bungled very badly.

VERAX

Cheltenham, 10th December, 1948

16

Johnny Foreigner

Rationing in Britain immediately invited comparisons of Britain's food lot with other nations. At the war's conclusion many saw a near-starving war-ravaged Europe as a grim reminder of the necessity of rationing. As time went by however more envied a Europe teeming with fruit, cheese, and chocolate.

The scarcity of good food in Britain roused the sentiment of 'why should we give foreigners our food when we have none?'. Xenophobic sentiment jostled alongside a genuine humanitarian concern for Europe, including humane treatment of Britain's former foe Germany.

Tea for Nazis

SIR – Is it not time we ceased treating our enemy as heroes? There are a few foolish people who, perhaps from humane considerations, think it necessary to dispense refreshment to Luftwaffe crews, who are lucky enough to land unscathed on our soil, in the course of raids against us.

Anything akin to inhumanity we deplore, but we apt to lose our sense of proportion. Have we so soon forgotten the recent Baedeker raids on our historic cities, and the unashamed gloating over this senseless destruction?

CHARLTONIAN

Cheltenham, 10th September, 1942

Fraternisation

SIR – On August Bank Holiday my wife and I were sitting in Ampthill Park overlooking the Bedfordshire War Agricultural Camp, when along came these Italians, who, after waiting about for a few minutes, were joined by three females from the camp. The meeting had obviously been arranged, and after 'pairing off' they proceeded down-hill towards Ampthill House. This incident was also witnessed with considerable disgust by three Army Cadets. A very fine example and encouragement!

A. .C. F

Bedford, 18th August, 1944

A Soldier's Complaint

SIR – I am one of the many soldiers stationed in a way-side village of Bedfordshire, and I find the hospitality of the publicans very poor. For instance, I walked into a public-housing where a publican was serving beer to his so-called regular customers, but refused me.

PTE A. H. SCOTT

Bedford, 18th August, 1944

Honoured Guests

SIR – Before the end of the war was near our government was promising strict punishment to every Nazi in Europe. Alas! The cry of the hungry German is more heartrending than the protests of our own housewives. Why not stop treating the Nazis like honoured guests? I wonder how the food officials dine, and the starving German, when shown on the cinema screen, they look just as well fed, if not better, than ourselves.

INDIGNANT

Dundee, 31st May, 1945

Snowball Wars'

SIR – Recently I saw a lively exchange of snowballing between British schoolboys and German P.O.Ws. Would-be future belligerents, before resorting to force, might well adopt a similar method of settling differences, rather than by employment of nuclear energy. Thus, future generations would mercifully be spared the degradation of austerity.

W. YOUNG

Leeds, 10th March, 1947

Belgian Chocolate

SIR – Last year I spent a month in Belgium and toured East and West Flanders and from the French to the Dutch Border. To say the Belgian working class has to exist on meagre rations is sheer nonsense. Rations in Belgium are greater than ours, and very much more can be bought off the ration. Petrol was freed last September. Furniture, carpets, lace curtains. Wallpaper, vacuum flasks and everything we need are there in abundance. Chocolates and sweets are now off the ration. The Belgians are working hard and are happy. Fruit is plentiful and cheap.

ALBERT KEEP

Leeds, 15th April, 1947

Rations for Europe

SIR – There would be some point in 'Grateful's' complaint if he could prove that those actually starving in Germany—and elsewhere in Europe—were the persons actually responsible for the attempt to starve this country into submission. He refers to the 'starving millions of Englishland'. I, for one, would like to know where these can be seen, for our present situation basic rations are quite sufficient to maintain us in perfect health, even those, who like myself, never eat 'off the rations'.

CHARLES DILTHY

Nottingham, 4th June, 1947

Be Thankful for Rationing

SIR – I have just returned from Spain, where I visited numerous ports including Barcelona and Bilbao. It was pitiful to see the crowd of beggars for food. They could not buy at the high prices that the well-to-do could pay. One poor woman on the quayside was rubbing her face, so I gave her two tablets of soap. The reason of my writing to you is to show how lucky we are to have rationing in England.

L.P. MELL, M.I. MECH. E.

Cheltenham, 28th July, 1947

Ex-Pilot Employer on Germans

SIR – I must reply to the letter from 'Disgusted' late of the R.A. I am an employer of a small group of German labourers, and I am on friendly terms with them as work is made easier that way. I can appreciate why some English farmers prefer them to British labour, as my men do not slack off when my back is turned, and their normal labour and overtime rates are cheaper than those for British labour. My German employees may spit in my face if they wish to when they go home, but I do not think they will.

EMPLOYER

Cheltenham, 28th July, 1947

Only British Beef

SIR – With reference to your leading article, 'The Fat and the Lean' the figures given by Mr A. V. Alexander are certainly interesting. Perhaps, however, we may be forgiven for not grumbling at our fighting men being given rations to keep them fighting fit. The real cause for the grumble is the ration of the 'Displaced Person'. These people are not wanted in their own country, so we accept them and give them 2s. 11d. worth of meat a week. After serving 24 years in the forces, I am left wondering who is of most value to my country.

ONLY BRITISH

Leeds, 9th December, 1947

War Biscuits

SIR – Mr. S. J. Britton, of 2, Mill Cottages Alderholt, asks for an explanation. Ordering biscuits from his grocer he was offered 'two squares of biscuits, in a very dilapidated condition, with foreign reading on it'. The grocer said that they were Italian – no points. The writer adds: 'I may be wrong, but I took it as an insult to bring them over and ask English people to eat what the Italians had left after we had been fighting them, getting shipping to bring them over when it is said there is a shortage of shipping to bring over what is really necessary'.

ANONYMOUS?

Yeovil, 12th December, 1947

Neutral Nourishment

SIR – Ireland, a neutral country, is giving to the hungry people of Europe thousands of tons of food. Switzerland, also neutral, could help and is nearer. In Britain, apart from those who have priority foods and those who can afford to eat out, people are not getting enough to eat, especially in the case of mothers of growing adolescents. They often go short of a meal. A weak cup of tea and wishful thinking is scarcely a meal for those who work the clock round.

TERESA TINSLEY

Nottingham, 11th October, 1945

Flooding Carrots

SIR – I read reports that 10,000 tons of Danish carrots are flooding the English market while our own farmers are having difficulty in disposing of much of their stock. May we expect, now that there is likely to be a surfeit of this vegetable, a spate of propaganda informing us of the benefit to be gained from the vitamins they contain?

This surely marks a new stage of ineptitude to which our food buyers have sunk. The farmer is to be encouraged to produce all he can—that is the Government's declared intention—and his reward is to see a flooded market.

H. F. JAMES

Hull, 26th January, 1948

17

Unfair Play

Many bemoaned the arbitrary nature of rationing, noting an increase in ration allowance one week only for it to be slashed the following month. Various professions vied with each other to mark themselves out as most worthy of additional rations. Factory workers complained of miners' extra rations while farmworkers felt short-changed for the heavy manual labour they undertook. The elderly demanded a bigger share while housewives constantly called for more rations for their young growing bairns. Local rivalries manifested as the neighbouring county, town, village or street seemed to be suspiciously endowed with fresh fruit, milk or whatever was in short supply. Bureaucracy was universally abhorred.

Tearful Climax

SIR – As Anti-Climax replied to my note I am of the opinion that she is not a working man's wife. I wrote and handed in my letter on Thursday afternoon, and on the following morning I went to the butcher's at 8 o'clock. He did not arrive till after 9 o'clock. A woman came in nearly in tears: she was, like myself, looking for food for her family. We are not the only ones, either, and I felt sorry for her.

How does Anti-Climax know that I haven't attended cooking demonstrations? Has Anti-Climax ever given a share to a less fortunate neighbour? Well, I have, and felt happy in in doing it? As for the tin-opener, I can only show tins of fruit and vegetables. As for porridge, we get it if we can get the milk and if we can get the milk it is not so bad for many dishes. Where can one obtain tripe? Only if a woman travels to town, and Anti-Climax wants to remember we have dinner at noon. I have volunteered for war service, but my husband tells me I am doing my duty at home. Which has it to be?

CLIMAX

Sunderland, 25th March, 1941

Factory Workers and Cheese

SIR – I cannot understand why miners and farm labourers need 7oz. more cheese than other workers. Although there are many factories which have canteens and supply meals, there are numerous others which have no canteens. I, like thousands of other workers in small factories, cannot get home for lunch, and therefore have to pack my food (1oz. of cheese). I appeal to local MPs to get this ration altered, say 5½oz. to minders and farms hands, 3½. to other workers.

R. HOROBIN

Nottingham, 7th April, 1941

Emergency Problems

SIR – I am writing for myself and others, who are engaged on work of national importance. The difficulty and trouble arises when one, residing in the rural district, for example, Hatfield Peverel, requires an emergency ration card. To obtain an emergency ration card, or, for that matter, anything connected with ration books, we are expected to go personally to the Rural District Food Office, Braintree, nine miles from here, the bus fare being 1s. 9d., after waiting about for buses. If unable to attend in person, you have to send your ration books and identity card by registered post, and if lucky you will receive your emergency ration card when it is too late. Now, come along, Parish Council of Hatfield

Peverel and try to make a sharper war effort.

J. M. MOORE

Chelmsford, 7th November, 1941

Farmers' Sons

SIR – It is useless to complain of the non-calling up of farmers' sons. Agriculture is a reserved occupation and therefore all key men in it have been retained on the land. Farming is at its quietest during the weeks immediately following Christmas. Nature cannot be hurried; neither can she be turned into a mass production factory. The farmer knows this and acts accordingly. During the waiting period time is filled by lambing, hedging, ditching, &c. Unfortunately, cows have a horrid habit of calving on the night one has planned to go to the pictures!

With regard to black market, I have seen no evidence of it in my district. Town dwellers should be careful not to judge all country people by the one or two they may meet.

FARMER'S DAUGHTER

Plymouth, 19th February, 1942

Teachers' Free Meals

SIR – Lest a misunderstanding should arise in the minds of the public of Barnstaple on the question of free meals for teachers, the teachers did not ask for free meals and reject the offer, but they assume that the offer was made because other authorities, including the Devon Country, make the same concession. 'The committee agreed, on the present numbers, to allow a meal free of charge to two teachers at each Feeding Centre provided that they remain on duty during the midday break'. Many authorities pay for this duty, but the teachers in the Barnstaple schools informed the Major that payment was not desired. The teachers bring the children from their schools to the Feeding Centre and supervise the meal. For this no teacher in Barnstaple receives either payment or a free meal. The circular of the

Board of Education stresses the point that all teachers are receiving a war bonus. This is not so. Only a proportion of the Barnstaple teachers receive any kind of bonus, and this is less than the amount agreed on by national agreement, and paid by all except six authorities.

It is felt that the ratepayers of Barnstaple do not know their teachers are working under worse conditions, both of pay and generally, than their colleagues under the Devon County Council and in the rest of the country.

R. G. CHUGG, BARNSTAPLE TEACHERS ASS.

Plymouth, 19th February, 1942

No Class Matter

SIR – It seems to be a great pity to try and make a class matter of what should be treated as a necessity. We are all prepared to stand a certain amount of suffering, but it is obviously not in the interests of mother or child to have more shock to the system than is absolutely necessary. If it would comfort 'Mother of One' to know it, I can assure her that, living in London as one of the hated 'well-to-do' I was left to bring an 11lb. baby into the world without anaesthetics for three nights and two days, and would willingly subscribe—and frequently do—to alleviate the suffering of anyone, and so would any of my well-to-do friends.

MOTHER OF THREE

Gloucester, 31st August, 1942

Maids Paradox

SIR – Can anyone explain to me why some people are allowed to have several maids between 18 and 30, while the aged and infirm have their only help called up even if she is over 40?

AGED AND INFIRM

Cheltenham, 10th September, 1942

Ration Books

SIR – May I suggest that all aggrieved and unsatisfied ration-book holders write at once to Lord Woolton, explaining the position and situation of residents of Southsea, Eastney, and Milton. Why have we a food office in Fawcett Road, also a very large secondary school, at present doing very little, the staff of which know enough of routine work to handle the work of issuing the new books?

S. C. WEEKS

Portsmouth, 12th May, 1943

Voluntarily Unfair

SIR – Mr. Tuck suggests that compulsory billeting would be unfair on people who 'genuinely could not and should not' take in evacuees. I suggest that voluntary billeting is unfair on the 'willing horse', and causes well-meaning people to be reluctant to throw open their homes when selfish people refuse to do so.

The danger of compulsory billeting is that it might be operated unfairly, but there is evidence to suggest that even under the present system coercion may be used in billeting evacuees on the working-class, while influential people get away scot-free.

What is needed is some attempt to 'ration' housing and some machinery to adjust differences which must occur even where people are reasonable, and to prevent cruelty on the part of landladies and carelessness on the part of evacuees.

Mr. Tuck also states that as there are many safe areas compulsory billeting is unnecessary. No doubt the lines of people waiting at the Billeting Office would be only too happy to hear of a safe space where accommodation is available.

ONLOOKER

Cheltenham, 13th July, 1944

Farce of Voluntary Billeting

SIR – Once again Cheltenham hits the headlines—this time in a Sunday paper—for its inhospitality to those in dire need. If only we could vow it was untrue! Let us be big enough to rise to it by cutting out the farce called voluntary billeting' which enable those with large houses and incomes to ignore all appeals, while smaller homes are forced to open their doors in the common sense of humanity. How about this for an advertisement for it. A woman worn out with street-tramping to find a bed after being bombed out, remarked to me 'I think Cheltenham must have more churches and less Christians than any other town in England'.

FACING FACTS

Cheltenham, 13th July, 1944

Full House

SIR – I expect the Londoners were terribly tired and fed up after the stress and horror of the bombs. I hope they now feel better and rested. I have eight evacuees and so many evacuee children (they are as good as gold) that I feel and sign myself.

THE OLD WOMAN WHO LIVED IN A SHOE

Cheltenham, 13th July, 1944

Well Fed Prisoners

SIR – Whatever may be the true condition of the peoples of Europe, our butter, margarine, and fats ration is ridiculously inadequate. Is the same type of mind responsible for this wretched rationing as it is responsible for the fish and coal mess? Is it necessary that our present rationing values should be so low? I think of the multitude of works canteens, school meals, and of certain restaurants, which are practically places of entertainment, serving unnecessary meals. I think of the gangs of our healthy prisoners feeding their faces at our expense.

When will the Food Ministry waken up and cater for the useful natives of this country.

FOOD FOR THOUGHT

Dundee, 8th June, 1945

Service Short Change

SIR – Having just returned from 2 ½ years' service abroad, I am surprised to find that the Service man on leave is not given the same equality as a civilian regarding food rationing. The following two points seem to require remedying: the civilian can purchase one packet of dried eggs per month; the service man, however, must produce eight 'egg' coupons, this being practically equivalent to one packet in two months. I was informed at the local food office that no sweet coupons are issued to personnel on leave, and that personal should obtain their ration from Service canteens. The latter arrangement is ridiculous. It is not practicable for personnel arriving in this country by air or sea to bring (if they can manage to obtain it) a month's supply of confectionary.

G. C. HEALEY, SUB.-LIEUT., R.N.V.R.

Hastings and St Leonards, 27th October, 1945

Our Scanty Food Rations

SIR – The energies of our Government seem mainly occupied with the atomic bomb, nationalisation of this and that, strikes, settling riots abroad, and the trail of war criminals.

We have won our victories here and abroad, but there is one enemy in our midst which is steadily gaining a footing, namely, malnutrition. For six years we have lived on the most frugal diet uncomplainingly. One person's weekly ration could easily be contained on an ordinary teaplate. Any doctor will tell you he was never so busy before, and the reason is undernourishment.

E. I. W.

Dundee, 23th November, 1945

Meagre Nourishment

SIR – It's a miracle how we exist on our meagre rations. Would it not be possible for the Food Minister to give one week's extra rations per four weeks' period to the single person and household of two? I have a household of five, but I admit it's easier cooking for five than one.

W. R. I. MEMBER

Dundee, 2nd December, 1946

Pointless

SIR – During the ration period which ended on Saturday the points value of certain goods was increased. The Minister of Food stated that this was done because of the greater demand for such commodities to ensure fairer distribution. On Saturday night we were informed that bread units could no longer be exchanged for points. So now we are back where we were before the vexed question on interchangeable bread units arose, but strangely enough, the increased points values are to remain, and in the case of dried eggs are to be raised a further two points. Against this, certain tinned goods are to be removed from the points list entirely. This would have been a comforting concession if the said goods were to be found on the grocers' shelves, but they are not. So once again the struggling housewife is left with the feeling that another fast one has been pulled on her.

M. H. J.

Dundee, 11th, December 1946

Jam Jealousy

SIR – With disgust I read that the Ministry of Food is to release 40,000 tons of jam and marmalade for catering only, at about 10 per cent below current retail prices, and will be in addition to the usual preserves allocation. Why should catering establishment etc. be allowed to have these preserves at all when the stuff is wanted in the home?

MORE JAM

Leeds, 25th March, 1947

Preservations

SIR – I got a sinking feeling when reading about 'Jam for caterers only'. If there is a surplus of jam, is it such a big thing to ask that we have it in the homes?

HUNGRY

Leeds, 25th March, 1947

Veggie Cartel

SIR – Many questions are being asked why the Government does not adopt price control on vegetable owing to the racket now being forced on the public. The public has the answer. Why not refuse to buy?

G. RICKETTS

Leeds, 25th March, 1947

Those Bought Cakes

SIR – Housewives should demand better quality cakes from shops. Bakers seem to take advantage of the fact that housewives have not sufficient fat to make their own cakes.

LONG SUFFERING

Nottingham, 27th April, 1948

Mean Ministry

SIR – It would seem that a locality, as well as certain sections of the public, do not get fair treatment from the Ministry of Food. We employ a number of fence erectors who are away from home all day, very rarely near a canteen or other place where they can obtain refreshments or meals. Although they are almost always working on farms, or building sites, we cannot obtain the extra cheese ration for them, because they have not the requisite letters on their unemployment books. When the Ministry recently granted additional ration to county building employees, we tried again, but without success, and it seems to us most unfair that whereas a farm labourer, who can often get home to meals, is allowed the extra cheese, our men must go without.

GERALD GILMER LTD

Lewes, 7th November, 1947

Potato Rationing

SIR – In view of potato-rationing and the consequent hardship to many households, would it not still be possible for many farmers who have not already sown out the potato fields with winter wheat to reharrow them and give local people a chance to gather the potatoes thus turned up? Many precious tons might be gained in this way for human or animal feeding.

HOUSEWIFE

Dundee, 12th November, 1947

Potato Too Far

SIR – We are wondering how, in the event of another dreadful winter, we shall obtain our meagre allowance of potatoes. Last year we were without a bus for six weeks, and had to hike 2½ miles over snowdrifts 10ft. high and in winds which almost cut pieces. We caught a train after waiting hours, and eventually arrived back without rations, completely exhausted, as it is uphill all the way. Please don't say we shall have to add potatoes to the burden.

WONDERING

Leeds, 25th November, 1947

Rations for One

SIR – In company with other members of Dundee Housewives' Association I had an interview with Mr Strachey, Minister of Food, some months ago on the question of better ration for persons living alone. His answer to us then was the same as that given to the old age pensioners—technical difficulties. I, and, I am sure, many others like me, am at a loss to understand the incapacity of a Government to solve such a small problem, a Government which has performed such marvels in so many other fields—coal, electricity, housing and food!

MRS JANE N. REID

Dundee, 29th September, 1948

Cornish Crime

SIR – I see by the Press that Cornish farmworkers are to have the aid of official snoopers to investigate their complaint that their supplementary rations are kept by their employers for their own use. In Cornwall they must receive something worth snooping for. The amount of rationed food I recently had permit for was: 10 ozs. Tea, 12 Ozs. Cheese, 1 lb. 8 ozs. Margarine, 1lb. 8ozs. Sugar, 1 lb. 6 ozs. Jam. This is the amount allowed for five farmworkers, and when I divide it, it has to last them six weeks.

The dividing of the 1 lb. 6. Ozs. Of jam into five portions is my big headache.

It certainly is about time that farmworkers were allowed to apply for and buy their own supplementary rations, as the obtaining and filling in of necessary forms, not to mention the buying and carrying home of the rations falls on the shoulders of the already over-worked.

FARMERS'S WIFE

Cheltenham, 9th October, 1947

Teacher Trauma

SIR – Your correspondent 'Concerned' must, I am afraid, consider the teaching profession consists of a group of beings of superhuman endurance and goodwill. The teacher, besides having the obvious task of imparting knowledge, has to be the milkman, the bank-clerk and the general nurse to her charges – and all this for a salary equivalent to the wages of an eighteen-year-old manual labourer! Yet 'Concerned' wishes the teachers to supervise, not only the school meal, but also the whole lunch—time break. In other words, the teacher has to do without his, or her, lunch hour.

If you want your children out of the cold and snow—which, I agree, is important – agitate with the Education Authority for a paid supervisor to keep them out of mischief in the school at lunchtime.

A. CAMEL

Aberdeen, 21st November, 1949

18

And Another Thing

Rationing affected businesses as much as customers. By 1945, for example, newspapers paper usage had been rationed to only 25% of their pre-war levels. In conjunction with pervasive censorship many complained that politicians were being given an easy ride on rationing by the press. George Orwell bemoaned the difficulties of being published at a time of paper shortage: 'Paper for books is so short that even the most hackneyed 'classic' is liable to be out of print, many schools are short of textbooks, new writers get no chance to start and even established writers have to expect a gap of a year or two years between finishing a book and seeing it published'. A few sung the praises of rationing and were content with their relative lot. Many more voices chimed in to the editors on issues as diverse as contaminated teacups to stolen rations and silent husbands. Rationed Britain teemed with stories, opinions and rumours waiting to be heard.

Foxes and Food Production

SIR – From the enclosed you will observe farmers state 'it should be made compulsory for all landowners and owners of woods to take measures to exterminate foxes on their land'. Many flock-masters know what happens to young lambs after birth straying from the mother's protection during hours of darkness. With the increasing corn area one dare not risk economically utilising shed corn on stubble and around corn ricks as poultry food. Daylight raids where foxes are harboured are inevitable. As one would expect in a fox-ridden area, we had two litters of cubs in standing corn last season. Corn farmers know what this means at harvest towards increased food production.

W. JAMES

Yeovil, 24th January, 1941

Grocer Simplification

SIR – Please allow me to voice the dissatisfaction of a grocer on the food rationing muddle. Surely the Food Office knew when they announced the rationing of jam that cheese was being considered as a ration food. It would have been much easier to have announced them both together and made one job of it. We are now faced with eight commodities rationed, which presents a task in itself making the books for a straight-forward customer who takes all her rationed goods at once, but it is definitely a test of patience at busy periods when faced with a customer with a number of ration books who has had several bits of each commodity during the week, and now wants to take the rest.

All this could have been alleviated if the public had been persuaded to deal at one shop for everything. No ration books would have been required—only a simple form stating that they wished to be rationed at a certain shop. The Food Office would know the amount to allow each shop, as they do now, and the grocer would allow the correct rations to each family, keeping only a small weekly register, to mark at the time of purchase. The saving in Food Office labour, printing, paper, money, time, and patience would be consid-erable.

A. A. W.

Leeds, 20th March, 1941

Letting Go

SIR – In regard to the letter appearing in your paper, entitled

'Unwelcome', there is another side to this question. We let
our rooms to a man and wife, out of kindness, as everyone
was asked to do, though we were later told we were in need of
the money, which is absurd. We have tried to make them
welcome and feel at home, but dirt and muddles do not agree
with cleanliness and tidiness.

ANOTHER ONCE BIT

Cheltenham, 21st March, 1941

Elusive 5s.

SIR – The recent correspondence how Civil Servants should
spend their 5s. cost-of-living bonus may now cease. Hardly
had the last note of the trumpets faded away when the Civil
Servants were informed that, as from Monday next, they
would be required to work three hours per week fewer than
hitherto; though presumably the same amount of work will
be expected of them. In the lower male clerical grade this
means a net loss of about 9d. a week; in higher grades, of
course, they are much worse off—all as a result of fighting to
get them a cost-of-living bonus.

A WORM ON THE TURN

Cheltenham, 21st March, 1941

Ungrateful and Selfish People

SIR – Maybe ungrateful and selfish people would be
interested to know that thousands of their menfolk worked
twelve hours a day in Germany on 100 per cent black bread
ration of 250 grammes per day, this being substituted at
times by potatoes. Dinner consisted each and every day of
one pint of cabbage soup, four potatoes, and a small amount
of gruel, such as that used by billposters. To these people I
say: 'Maybe then this food rationing would not appear too
bad after all.'

JOHN HENRY BRADENS. LATE P.O.W. NO. 32692.

Plymouth, 8th July, 1946

Truth Waiting for Extra Pages

SIR – Your Saturday night leader contained this to my unsubtle mind, confusing sentence: 'But in spite of what certain Ministers and MPs think or say about bold bad barons, it is the newsprint which has been rationed by the Government, not the news by the newspapers'. Correct me if I am wrong, but I thought that what was in question in the 'Freedom of the Press' controversy was not the quantity of newsprint issued, but the quality of the news issued. If we are to understand that the truth has been waiting for extra pages, the 'bold bad barons' will be looking forward to giving us facts with their translations.

J. E. PORRIT

Hartlepool, 26th August, 1946

Socialist Utopia

SIR – With twelve months of peace behind us, and with a strong Socialist Government in power, we are still faced with two major domestic problems. We are faced with even greater shortages. Our milk ration has just been cut down again. The bacon ration is now less than during the worst years of the war, and whoever thought that bread, the staff of life, would become the concern of the ration book weary housewife? At a recent by-election the country was proudly informed that they were to be presented with a further two ounces of sweets per head in October. A cheaper form of vote cadging has yet to be experienced.

Mr Aneurin Bevan is taking a rest in Switzerland. We all trust he will return to the fold displaying even greater vigour to stamp out the last vestige of private enterprise left in the building industry. Many homeless Britons will be ushered into prefabricated houses or broken-down Army camps. The returning service man, after six years of fighting across the deserts of Africa, the steaming jungles of Burma, fighting in the air and on the sea, will be presented upon demobilisation with a residence for his wife and family. But imagine his consternation when he finds it is the tin hunt which his comrades so recently vacated.

MALCOLM WOOD

Cheltenham, 3rd September, 1946

Same Old

SIR – After the Great War the world was bulging with food, but the pockets of the people were empty of money with which to purchase this much needed 'abundance'. SO wheat and coffee were burned, fish thrown back into the sea, Nature's bounty restricted by 'subsidies' to farmers to grow less food and the ships designed to distribute the stuff to those clamouring to consume it were broken up. This is called 'over-production'. Today, after the World War, on a the 'planners' have ensured that the pockets of the people are bulging with useless £ notes, but there is nothing to buy. This is called 'world food shortage'—so what?

NORMAN BURCHETT

Plymouth, 2nd September, 1947

Waste Paper

SIR – I was surprised to read that the newspaper industry is to be handicapped by the shortage of paper. One would imagine that the Government, which, by poster, pamphlet, and form, is so lavish with paper, would allocate sufficient numbers. Why is paper allowed to be so casually destroyed? Look at any dump around Cheltenham, where heaps and heaps of paper are thrown away all through the year. For one instance, at pits in Sandylane paper of all kinds and colours is being buried, in addition to wood, rubber, and metal. For 20 feet deep and more the pits are being filled with such material.

EGBERT GREGORY

Cheltenham, 9th January, 1948

Bad Old Days

SIR – I have been astonished at some letters about the 'good old days'. The writers seem to have forgotten all about unemployment, with plenty of bacon and eggs in the shops and the poor working man with insufficient money to buy them. I say the good old days are here now. Let's keep them.

WORKING BOY

Nottingham, 6th September, 1948

Bountiful Harvest

SIR – Regarding the meagreness of the harvest ration of which Mrs Clark complains, these are supplementary to the ordinary ration. Strangely enough, I have yet to hear a complaint from the recipients. As their (nowadays) good wages carry with them perquisites in the shape of four pints of milk daily, potatoes, oatmeal and flour, and they usually have hens, often a pig, and invariably a well-stocked vegetable garden, I don't think they are likely to suffer from malnutrition. Regarding those awful forms, I reckon them roughly in the region of 20 annually. As some of them bring a reward in the shape of hard cash, I can't imagine any hard-headed farmer resisting such a bargain, of whatever rationalist his conscience. We are not living in Utopia, but who wants to, anyway?

NAE BOTHER

Dundee, 25th September, 1948

Places

Aberdeen: *Aberdeen Journal*
Aylesbury: *Bucks Herald*
Barnstaple: *North Devon Journal*
Bedford: *Bedfordshire Times and Independent, Bedfordshire Times & Standard*
Berwick upon Tweed: *The Berwick Advertiser, Berwickshire News and General Advertiser*
Burnley: *Burnley Express*
Chelmsford: *Chelmsford Advertiser*
Cheltenham: *Gloucestershire Echo, Gloucester Citizen, Cheltenham Chronicle*
Chesterfield: *Derbyshire Times and Chesterfield Herald*
Derby: *Derby Daily Telegraph*
Dover: *Dover Express*
Dundee: *Dundee Courier, Dundee Evening Telegraph, Sunday Post*
Gantham: *Grantham Journal*
Gloucester: *Gloucestershire Times*
Hartlepool: *Hartlepool Mail*
Hastings and St Leonards: *Hastings and St Leonards Observer*
Hull: *Hull Daily Mail*
Kirkcaldy: *Fife Free Press & Kirkcaldy Guardian*
Leeds: *Yorkshire Post and Leeds Intelligencer: Yorkshire Evening Post*
Lewes: *Sussex Agricultural Express*
Lichfield: *Lichfield Mercury*
Lincoln: *Lincolnshire Echo*
Nottingham: *Nottingham Evening Post*
Plymouth: *Western Morning News*
Portsmouth: *Portsmouth Evening News*
Preston: *Lancashire Evening Post*
Redhill: *Surrey Mirror*
Selkirk: *Southern Reporter*
Sunderland: *Sunderland Daily Echo and Shipping Gazette*
Taunton: *Taunton Courier, and Western Advertiser*
Wells: *Wells Journal*
Yeovil: *Western Gazette*